The
POPULAR MECHANICS
Home Book of
REFINISHING FURNITURE

The

POPULAR MECHANICS

Home Book of

REFINISHING FURNITURE

by Arthur Mikesell

A POPULAR MECHANICS PRESS BOOK

HAWTHORN BOOKS, Inc.

PUBLISHERS
NEW YORK

First Edition, June, 1963
Second Printing, May, 1965
Third Printing, October, 1966
Fourth Printing, June, 1967

4586

ACKNOWLEDGMENTS

Two members of the *Popular Mechanics* magazine staff were particularly helpful in the preparation of this book: Mr. W. Clyde Lammey, Associate Shop and Crafts Editor, who supplied valuable information on a number of finer points and read the manuscript for technical accuracy; Mr. John Jefchek, *Popular Mechanics* cabinetmaker, formerly Shop Instructor at the Chicago Art Institute, who aided the author by making available the knowledge and experience gained during his many years of specialized work in the finishing field.

Space limitations prevent mentioning all the individuals whose enthusiastic co-operation made this book possible; however, the following companies were especially helpful in supplying technical information and photographs:

Adelphi Paint and Color Works, Inc.
Adjustable Clamp Company
Albert Constantine and Son, Inc.
Albertson and Company
American Brush Manufacturers Association
Bahr-Manning Company
Benjamin Moore and Company
Black and Decker Manufacturing Company
Burgess Vibrocrafters, Inc.
Campbell-Hausfeld Company
The Carborundum Company
Chicago Bronze and Color Works
Consolidated Chemical and Paint Corp.
Cook Paint and Varnish Company
David Linzer and Sons, Inc.
Delta Power Tool Division of Rockwell
    Manufacturing Company
Desmond Brothers
Devcon Corporation
De Vilbiss Company
Dremel Manufacturing Company
E. I. du Pont de Nemours and Company
Elliot Paint and Varnish Company
Forest Products Laboratory, U.S.D.A.
Georgia-Pacific Corporation
Gillespie Varnish Company
The Glidden Company
Grand Rapids Varnish Corporation
James B. Sipe and Company
Klean-Strip Company, Inc.
Krylon Company
Magicolor Company
Masonite Corporation
Minnesota Mining and Manufacturing Co.

Minwax Company
National Chemical and Manufacturing Co.
National Paint, Varnish and Lacquer
    Association
The O'Brien Corporation
Otto Bernz Company, Inc.
Parker Manufacturing Company
Pierce and Stevens Chemical Corporation
Plasti-Kote, Inc.
Pratt and Lambert, Inc.
Red Devil Tools, Inc.
Samuel Cabot, Inc.
Sapolin Paints, Inc.
Sargent-Gerke Company
Savogran Company
Sears, Roebuck and Company
Seidlitz Paint and Varnish Company
Sherwin-Williams Company
Skil Corporation
Stanley Power Tools
    (Division of the Stanley Works)
Thor Power Tool Company
Turner Corporation
United States Plywood Corporation
Vita-Var Corporation
Weldit, Inc.
Western Pine Association
William Zinsser and Company, Inc.
Wilson-Imperial Company
Woodfinishing Products Company
Woodhill Chemical Company
Wooster Brush Company
W. P. Fuller and Company
W. R. Brown Corporation

The acknowledgments for this book would not be complete without giving credit to my very tolerant wife, who patiently allowed her dining room to be littered with research material, her prized black walnut dining table to be used as a desk and who, in addition, retyped the entire manuscript in triplicate.

Contents

Introduction

The term "refinishing" has many meanings:

A young housewife buys a secondhand chest, cleans it, removes the old finish, and then applies a coat of bright synthetic enamel. After she has added shining new hardware to the chest, it will give yeoman's service in the children's room for years. This is an example of "refinishing," and the whole job took only one day.

The couple next door spend three weeks renovating a dry sink they discovered in a farmer's attic. They strip off six coats of paint, sand the surface smooth, apply a wash coat of shellac, and top it with a hand-rubbed wax finish. This is also "refinishing."

Regardless of the amount of work involved or the time consumed in the project, most people refinish furniture for reasons of economy. Few newlyweds can afford all new furniture for their first apartment. Also, they usually inherit a number of pieces which are not adaptable to their decorating scheme. Refinishing blends old furniture with new surroundings, and the work involved turns them into integrated parts of the new household. In fact, these refinished pieces often gain a sentimental place-of-honor when the couple finally move into their first house.

In addition to the money to be saved by refinishing old furniture, a great deal of satisfaction can be gained from a successful refinishing project, whether it is a painstaking restoration of an antique or simply the refurbishing of a cast-off. Even the most unattractive piece of furniture can usually be restyled and refinished so that it is serviceable and decorative. Many people begin such projects to save money and then discover that refinishing can also be a rewarding hobby. Often, it advances from the hobby stage to become a source of extra income.

Many books in the finishing and refinishing field are written for the reader who has a good general knowledge of the whole field of woodworking. This book, however, includes complete background material, making it a comprehensive, detailed, and illustrated guide which is ideal for the novice, and is also a handy reference book for general shop use by even the most experienced craftsman.

ARTHUR M. MIKESELL

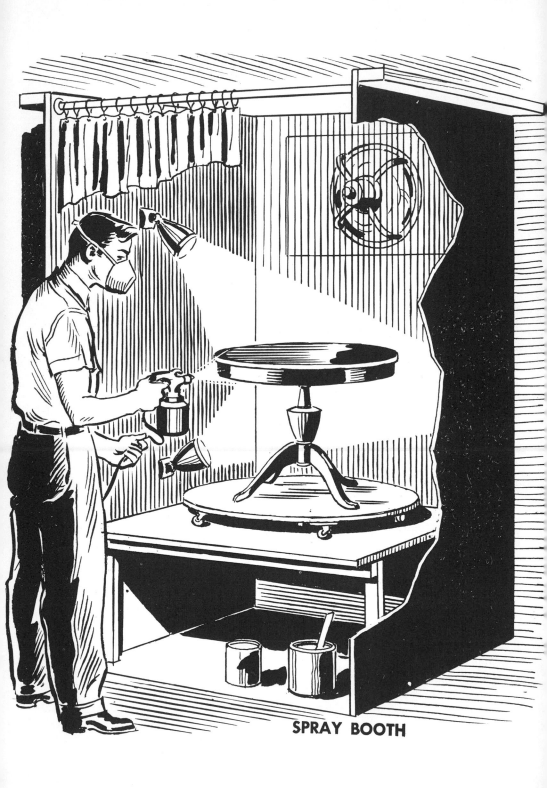

SPRAY BOOTH

I

Before You Begin

SPRAY VERSUS BRUSH APPLICATION

No elaborate array of equipment is needed to turn out a first-class job of refinishing, but the job is half-finished if the right tools are available, and you have a knowledge of how they should be used. Because a proper beginning is so important, this first chapter is devoted to choosing the proper tools, using them correctly, and caring for them after they have been used.

Although spray guns and finishing materials which are packaged in aerosol cans are becoming more popular, brushes are acceptable and often necessary tools for proper application of finishing materials. It takes more time to apply enamel to a chest by brush than it does to apply it by spray, but the actual finishing preparations are simpler. Just spread a layer of newspapers on the floor, thin the enamel to proper consistency, and you are ready to begin.

When applying enamel by spray, however, it is necessary to make provisions to catch the overspray. Ideally, the piece of furniture should be placed inside a three-sided enclosure to catch stray paint, which is called a spray booth. The finishing material must be strained, then thinned to spraying consistency. In addition, the spray gun must be scrupulously clean and properly adjusted.

Many beginners have misconceptions regarding these methods of applying finish, feeling that spray application is a complicated and delicate process which should be done only by professionals, but that any beginner can slap on finish with a brush. The spray process is actually simpler and much faster than brush application, especially when quick-drying materials are used, because of the brush marks created by using such finishes. But brush application is traditional and retains its popularity because it is relatively easy, and the low cost of the equipment required is slight.

11

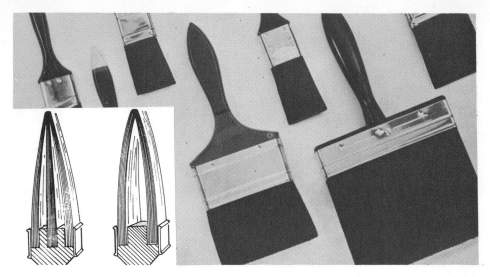

BRUSHES

Over twenty-five different types of brushes are on the market. Each type is available in several different sizes, and they are available in a wide range of raw materials, bristle lengths, quality, and contents.

A brush consists of rows or thicknesses of bristles set in rubber, or in a similar adhesive. These bristles are clamped in a metal ferrule along with the filler block, which is usually a part of the handle. Usually the number of bristle rows in a brush is stamped on the handle in a simple code, for example, "XX" for a double row, "XXX" for a triple row. Cheaper brushes, which are not intended for fine work, have a large filler block and less bristles. Single- or double-row brushes have less body, and are especially useful for jobs which require flexibility.

Brushes are also available in varying bristle lengths; those with longer bristles hold more finish. The bristles of quality brushes are straight, reasonably uniform in diameter (for even resiliency) and have split ends which form a number of *flags* or thin filaments. Many refinishers and restorers still prefer brushes made from animal bristles, but nylon and other synthetic bristles with flagged ends are acceptable for most refinishing.

For applying free-flowing, quick-drying materials such as varnishes and shellac, softer brushes are best. Such brushes are made of goat, sable, badger, or skunk bristles. At one time the most popular bristles for soft brushes were obtained from the fitch (the polecat of Europe). These brushes were called fitch-hair brushes, and were sometimes described as fitch-flowing brushes. However, most brushes which carry this name today are made of bristles from the American skunk.

The finest general-purpose brushes were once made from hog bristles, which were imported from China in great quantities. But these bristles are no longer imported in quantity, and today most general-purpose brushes contain only one per cent of the China bristles, blended with horsehair or other kinds of bristle. They are usually labeled *China Blend.* Although these brushes are acceptable for many purposes, they should not be confused with brushes made only from China bristle, which are of much better quality. True China bristle is pure black: this information is not a significant distinction since most black, bristle found today is actually an off-white bristle which has been dyed black, and is of a lower quality. The best animal bristle presently available is imported from Europe; it is also an off-white but has a golden cast. The poorest quality animal bristle is horsehair which wears down quickly and, consequently, is used only in utility-grade brushes.

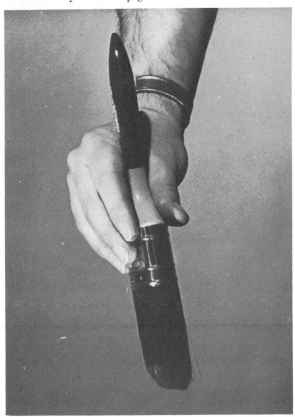

Above and *right:* A narrow (two-inch) chisel-edge, best for finishing work. Flag tips of bristles hold paint. Longest bristles form a sharp line for accuracy in painting.

The best brush to use for most finishing work is from two to two-and-a-half inches wide, and has three rows of high-quality flagged bristles. It has a tapering edge, which is referred to as either a chisel, or chisel-cut, edge, depending on the type of formation used for the wedge shape. In the very best brushes the bristles are arranged to form a chisel edge. This makes it possible to cut a sharply defined line with a corner of the brush, which is essential in some brush finishing.

Several simple tests should be made before a brush is purchased:

1. Check the ends of the bristles for flags.
2. Spread the bristles apart and examine the filler block; a brush which has an unusually thick block is usually the cheap utility type, which is not suitable for finishing.
3. Check the handle to determine what type of bristles have been used in the brush.
4. Grasp a one-inch section of bristles at one edge, and pull them to one side. Good bristles spring back into position when released.
5. Press the brush gently against a smooth surface. The edge of a good brush will form a sharp, even line which has little or no flare.
6. Clasp the ends of the bristles firmly and give them a sharp tug. If too many bristles pull out, it indicates that a poor adhesive has been used; however, even the best brushes have a few loose bristles.

Unless all new brushes are conditioned before they are used, the bristles will absorb materials from the finish which makes them stiffen. This lessens the normal resiliency and impairs efficiency. To condition a brush properly, it should first be wrapped in heavy Kraft paper as if it were to be put into storage. It should then be suspended in a can or brush keeper which contains enough linseed oil to cover the full length of the bristles for a period of at least 24 hours before it is to be used.

Before using the brush, the excess linseed oil should be removed by pressing the bristles against a flat surface. The brush should then be held between the palms of your hands, and twirled inside an empty can in order to remove the remaining oil. Then the bristles should be dipped in turpentine several times, and the excess turpentine should be removed in the same manner as the linseed oil was removed. The bristles should then be combed with a steel comb and smoothed to remove the channels or ridges formed by the comb. It is especially important to make sure that all the linseed oil has been removed, since even a small amount will act as a retarder when mixed with some finishing materials. In order to make sure that all oil has been removed,

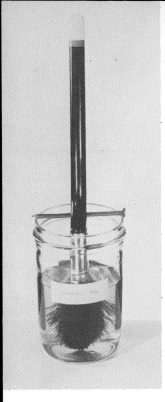

Brush should be conditioned in linseed oil (*left*). Oil can then be removed by spinning the brush rapidly (*above*). Dip brush about one-third its length into finishing liquid (*right*). Scraping the bristles on rim (*below*) damages brush.

the brush should be dipped in the finish, and then brushed over a rough surface several times before the work is actually begun. This will also remove any loose bristles.

Certain brush techniques are always applicable. When applying any finishing material with a brush, the bristles should be dipped into the finish so that it covers only a little over one-third their length. The excess should be tapped off against the inside of the can, or on a strike wire which is easily fitted into the top of the can. When finishing a wide horizontal surface, application is first started at the center and then worked toward the edges. A brushing stroke should always begin with a loaded brush on the unfinished area moving toward any area to which finish has just been applied. This is especially important with shellac, varnish, and other fast-drying materials which must be flowed on and allowed to level off without undue brushing. When materials are being applied on a vertical surface, the material should be flowed on with vertical strokes and finished horizontally with the unloaded brush to insure even coverage and prevent sags, runs, and "holidays," skipped spots or places covered with only a thin film. To avoid drips, which occur when you stroke a loaded brush over an edge, work from the center to the edge. To finish round objects, it is best to brush around and finish off with light, lengthwise strokes.

Finish should never be applied in an inside corner by pressing a brush full of material into the corner. Instead, a partially dry brush should be eased into the corner and drawn out lightly. On large surfaces, only a narrow strip

To assure even coat, wipe brush on strike-wire (*above*), paint from wet to dry (*right*).

is worked at a time so that each stroke brushes back to a wet edge. A heavily loaded brush should never be used to finish a groove or carving. The material will fill depressions, and take days, possibly weeks, to dry. Plan the brush strokes to end at high spots or sharp edges.

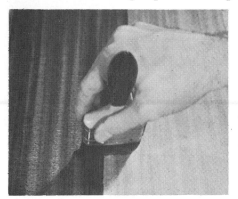

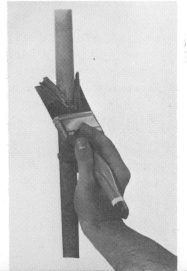

Above left: Strokes must lap evenly to avoid holidays or skipping. *Above right:* If brushes are overloaded (top left picture) paint will run, drip, or splatter. *Below right:* Brushing over raised edges, slots causes running. *Below left:* This causes fishtailing. On all narrow turnings use small brush or horizontal strokes.

Each of the following conditions is caused by misuse of a brush in some way:

Shedding in a good brush is usually caused by excessive bending of the bristles during cleaning. Too much wringing or slapping of the brush against a hard surface will cause the bristles to break off just below the ferrule.

Flaring is due to an accumulation of hardened finishing material at the heel of the brush caused by overloading the bristles or dipping the brush too deep in the finishing material. A brush in this condition may have to be treated with a paint softener or discarded in some instances.

Loose handles result from allowing a brush to soak in water so long that the handle swells and spreads or breaks the ferrule. When the wood shrinks after drying, the handle becomes loose.

Fingering frequently results from using the side of the brush to cover narrow surfaces rather than switching to a smaller brush.

If a refinishing job is interrupted, the brush may be left in the finishing material for a short time to keep it from hardening. However, if the job is to be postponed for more than an hour, the brush should be wrapped in aluminum foil twisted tightly around the handle to keep the brush moist. With paint and some other finishing materials, a brush can be stored overnight by simply wrapping it in foil, or one of the new chemical brush "keepers" which prevent the finishing material in the brush from hardening can be used.

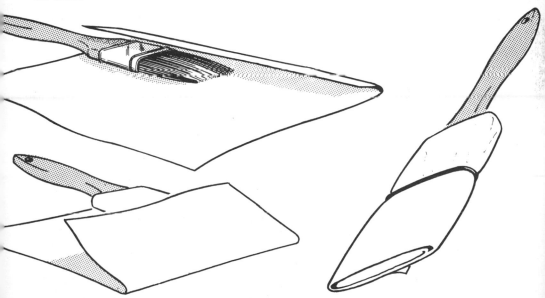

Brushes will harden if left in finishing material for more than brief periods. If a job is halted temporarily, wrap brushes well in aluminum foil or store in a chemical keeper.

Left: Using the side of a brush on narrow surfaces where a small brush is required will cause bristles to "finger." *Above:* For complete cleaning, solvent must be worked into a brush's heel with the hands.

A brush should be cleaned in the proper solvent for the material in which it has been used. If enamel, varnish, or oil stain or oil paint have been used, the brush should be cleaned in turpentine, or one of the special cleaning solvents now available. Lacquer thinner is used to clean lacquer brushes, and denatured alcohol for brushes used in alcohol, stain, or shellac. Water-stain brushes should be washed in warm water and dipped in a vinegar solution. To assure thorough cleaning, the solvent should be worked through the bristles and into the heel of the brush with the hand. The excess solvent is then removed, as was the linseed oil when it was used for conditioning.

For dry storage, condition and clean brushes with solvent and wrap in heavy Kraft paper.

Paint and varnish brushes may be stored safely for a time by suspending them in a solvent mixture or by coating with a chemical brush keeper, following the instructions given on the container, if the same brushes are to be used again within a month or so. For paint brushes, a fifty-fifty mixture of turpentine and raw linseed oil can be used; a fifty-fifty mixture of varnish

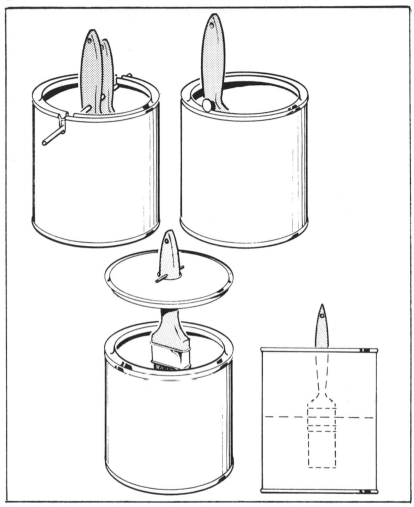

The safest method for temporary storage of paint brushes—not for permanent storage—is a device easily constructed at home, as shown *above*. Bristles should never be allowed to touch the bottom and should be stored only in the solution proper for bristle and paint.

and turpentine can be used for varnish or enamel brushes. Shellac and lacquer brushes should be stored dry. If the ends of the bristles rest on the bottom of a container, they will be permanently bent. The liquid level should also be checked periodically to make sure that the bristles are fully submerged. For long periods of storage, the brushes must be cleaned thoroughly in a solvent, wrapped in oiled paper or foil, and sealed with tape.

Handles and bristles of encrusted brushes can be reclaimed with steel brushing and combing.

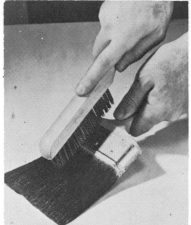

SPRAY EQUIPMENT

The recent development of portable spray guns of quality which are priced within the reach of home craftsmen has had much to do with the growing use of spray guns for refinishing. As previously mentioned, spraying is the fastest method of applying a finishing material. Also, materials applied with a spray gun usually dry more quickly.

Good results can be obtained with paint-spray attachments for vacuum cleaners. The handy, lightweight spray units with built-in, vibrator-type motors are economical and do acceptable work. One type has a triple-nozzle turret providing a fan spray for large flat surfaces, a circular spray for small articles, and a fog spray for use with insecticides.

For spray-finishing small items—workshop power tools, picture frames, chairs, lamp tables and the like—the aerosol can enjoys mounting popularity. No cleaning is required; there is very little waste, and there is no thinning or straining of finishing materials. The nozzle is aimed at the object to be sprayed and the button pressed; it is almost as simple as that. When the can is empty, it can be thrown away. These features make the aerosol can a comparatively expensive means of applying a finish, but many finishers and re-finishers feel that the added convenience is worth the extra cost.

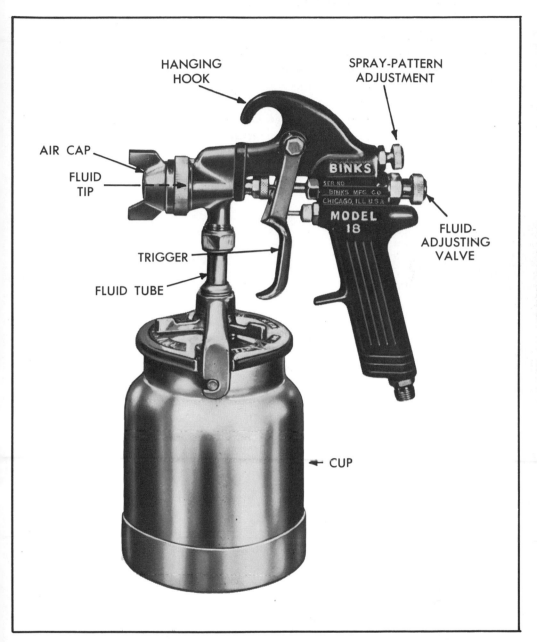

HANGING HOOK

SPRAY-PATTERN ADJUSTMENT

AIR CAP

FLUID TIP

BINKS

SER NO
BINKS MFG CO
CHICAGO, ILL. U.S.A.

MODEL 18

FLUID-ADJUSTING VALVE

TRIGGER

FLUID TUBE

CUP

Spray guns vary in the ways by which paint is fed to the nozzle. In a *suction-feed* gun (sometimes called siphon-feed), air passing over the fluid tip causes a partial vacuum, and atmospheric pressure entering the paint cup through a hole in the cover forces the finishing material up through the fluid line into the air stream. In a *pressure-feed* gun, part of the air is diverted to the closed paint container and forces the paint to the fluid tip. A pressure-feed gun is capable of spraying heavier liquids than is possible with a suction-feed gun.

Once the finishing material arrives at the air cap, it may be mixed with the air either inside or outside the cap. Internal-mix air caps are found only on pressure-feed guns and have a single narrow slot. External-mix caps have three holes, one in the center and one in the end of each of the two "horns" which are located above and below the center hole. External-mix caps are used both on pressure-feed and suction guns. Paints formulated for brush application can be sprayed with a pressure-feed gun. Some paints come in both brushing and spraying consistencies; however, ordinary paints and lacquers should be thinned for spraying with suction-feed guns.

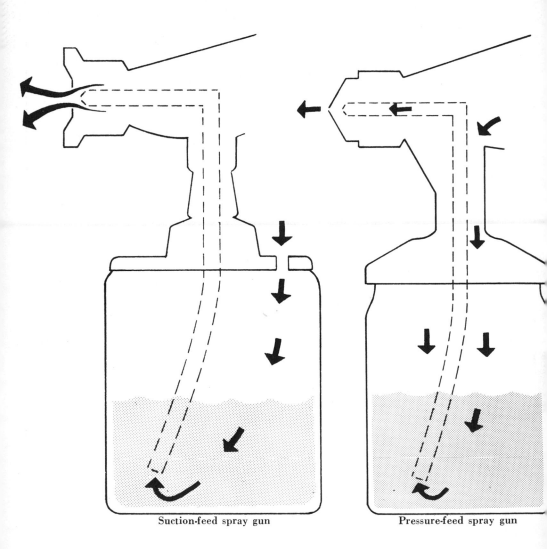

Suction-feed spray gun   Pressure-feed spray gun

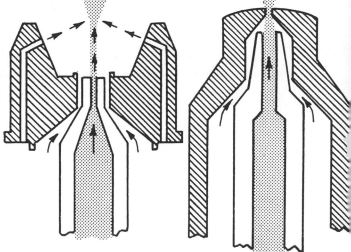

Pressure-feed sprayer (*above*) uses metal cap. Diagrams show external-mix (*center*) and internal-mix type sprayer caps.

Guns that operate directly from small air compressors which have no pressure-controlling device are of the bleeder type and pass air at all times to prevent a pressure build-up in the air lines. Non-bleeder guns are used on controlled-pressure lines, with the trigger controlling both air and paint flow.

Compressors may be of either the diaphragm or piston type. The former is less expensive and will serve all the needs of most amateur refinishers. The inexpensive diaphragm will last for many hours and is simple to replace. Piston-type compressors are generally used for heavy-duty work.

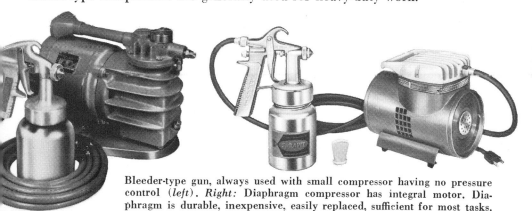

Bleeder-type gun, always used with small compressor having no pressure control (*left*). *Right:* Diaphragm compressor has integral motor. Diaphragm is durable, inexpensive, easily replaced, sufficient for most tasks.

As a rule, finishing materials should be sprayed at a temperature of seventy degrees or higher since the viscosity of a cold finishing material often makes it difficult to spray. The fluid to be sprayed should be strained through a sixty-mesh screen or a piece of nylon hose to make sure that it contains no particles which may clog the nozzle.

For comfort and safety, a respirator should be used when spraying. As an additional safety precaution, spray should never be used in a room where

Left: Small turret-nozzle guns provide three spray patterns.
Right: Spray attachment for vacuum cleaners is useful device.

there is an open flame. Because nearly all finishing materials are highly flammable, adequate ventilation should be provided: an exhaust fan to force fumes outside is the preferred means of ventilation. Objects not to be sprayed should be removed from the room, or covered, to prevent overspray from being deposited on them. When more than an occasional spraying job is planned, it is worthwhile to construct a ventilated spray booth in the corner of a basement. However, a spray booth must meet certain safety codes, and it may be simpler and cheaper to take the work outside on a suitable drying day.

NYLON
HOSIERY

RUBBER
BAND

Before filling gun, strain paint (*right*); when spraying use respirator—for safety and comfort.

Skill in handling a spray gun can be acquired by practicing on newspapers taped to the side of a large carton, experimenting with the full range of adjustment, starting from the nearly-closed nozzle position that produces a pattern about one inch wide when the trigger is pulled back fully. Some spray guns produce a fan-shaped spray, some a round pattern; still others can be adjusted for either pattern. The longer dimension of an oval pattern is referred to as its width.

As the gun is adjusted for a wider pattern and the flow of liquid increased, atomization becomes coarser. The gun should be held so that the nozzle is from six to eight inches from the working surface. A pattern about six inches wide is usually right for spraying most flat surfaces. For turnings or small surfaces the pattern should be narrower. Holding the gun too close to the work will cause a heavier deposit of paint in a small area unless the speed of stroking is increased.

To produce a coating of uniform thickness on a vertical surface, the gun is aimed so that the axis of the spray cone is at right angles to the work surface. On each stroke, the gun should be moved parallel to the work with a free-arm movement, flexing the wrist at the ends of the stroke. Each stroke

Right: One easy rule of thumb is good enough for measuring proper distance between piece and sprayer — about one-half foot. Spray gun should be held with the spray cone always at right angle to surface, if it is a vertical plane (*below*). Angle changes for horizontal spraying paint jobs.

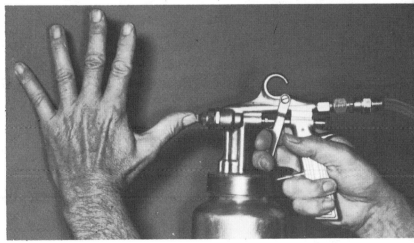

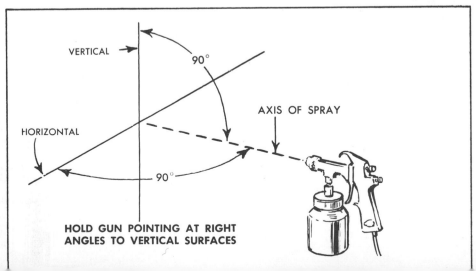

VERTICAL

HORIZONTAL

90°

90°

AXIS OF SPRAY

HOLD GUN POINTING AT RIGHT ANGLES TO VERTICAL SURFACES

should overlap the previous one from thirty to fifty per cent, just enough to give a film of uniform thickness.

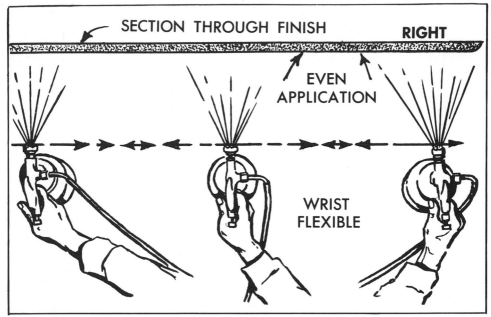

Hold neither the wrist nor the elbow stiff when painting with a spray gun (*above and below*). This rule is true not only for vertical surfaces, but also for horizontal surfaces.

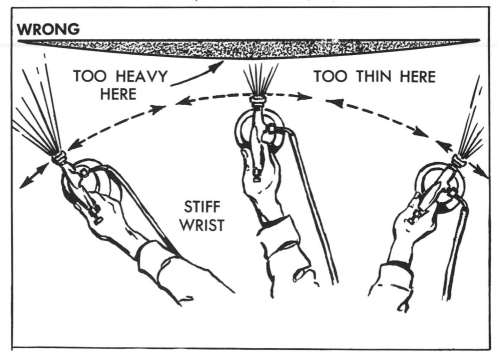

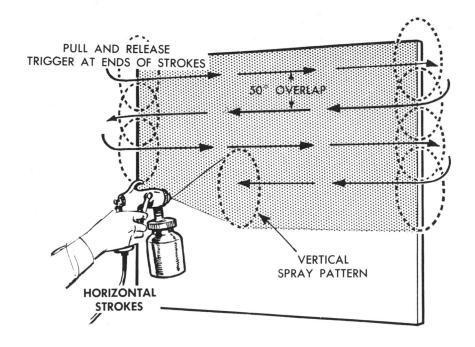

PULL AND RELEASE
TRIGGER AT ENDS OF STROKES

50° OVERLAP

VERTICAL
SPRAY PATTERN

HORIZONTAL
STROKES

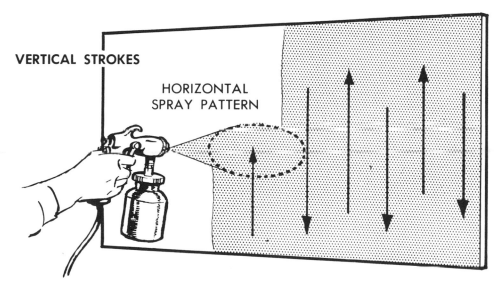

VERTICAL STROKES

HORIZONTAL
SPRAY PATTERN

To coat a panel with horizontal strokes, the nozzle should be adjusted to produce a vertical spray pattern in order to make consecutive strokes in opposite directions. On long, narrow panels the strokes can be made vertically, with the nozzle adjusted to produce a horizontal pattern. When spraying large surfaces where horizontal strokes must be overlapped, the ends of the strokes are feathered. Similar feathering of adjacent strokes will build up the paint coat to proper thickness at the overlap.

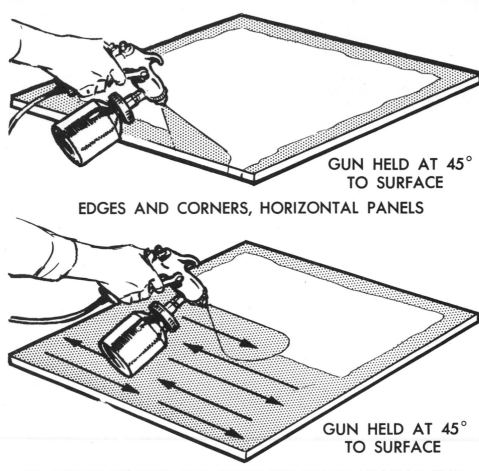

GUN HELD AT 45°
TO SURFACE

EDGES AND CORNERS, HORIZONTAL PANELS

GUN HELD AT 45°
TO SURFACE

TO COVER HORIZONTAL SURFACES START AT NEAR END

On large horizontal surfaces, such as table tops, the edges and corners are sprayed first, holding the gun at a 45-degree angle. Then the center area is sprayed. To finish an inside corner, it is usually best to work one side first, then the other. When applying clear finishing materials or stain to an inside corner, each side must be coated separately to obtain an even color.

If it is necessary to tilt a gun to spray the underside of shelving or similar materials, the cup should not be more than half full so that it can be tilted without the finishing material reaching the lid. On most guns, the position of the fluid tube can be changed so that it continues to feed in this tilted position. A small spray pattern is best for furniture finishing as it permits close control of overspray. A turntable which can be used to hold the work will permit easier handling and make all parts accessible.

To minimize overspray on an area already coated, all the edges and concealed surfaces should be done first. Turnings should be sprayed with vertical strokes and a horizontal spray pattern adjusted so that it is slightly wider

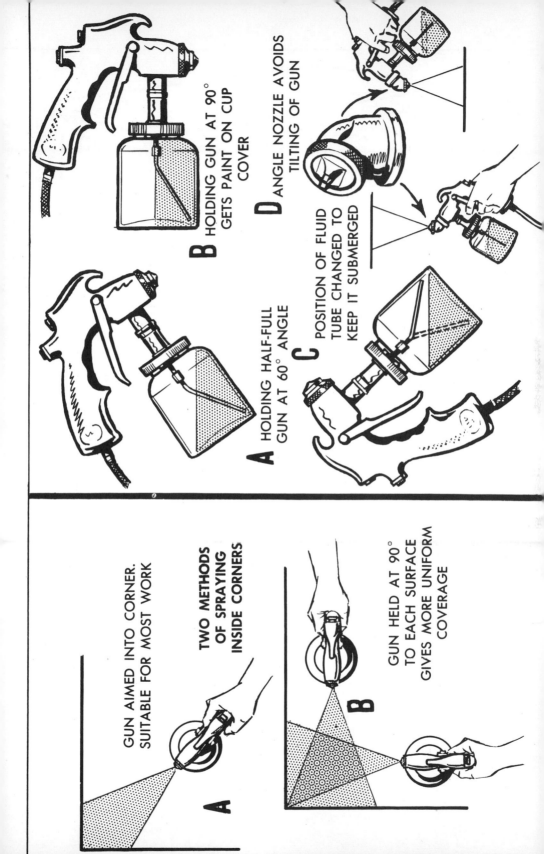

B HOLDING GUN AT 90° GETS PAINT ON CUP COVER

D ANGLE NOZZLE AVOIDS TILTING OF GUN

A HOLDING HALF-FULL GUN AT 60° ANGLE

C POSITION OF FLUID TUBE CHANGED TO KEEP IT SUBMERGED

GUN AIMED INTO CORNER. SUITABLE FOR MOST WORK

TWO METHODS OF SPRAYING INSIDE CORNERS

A

GUN HELD AT 90° TO EACH SURFACE GIVES MORE UNIFORM COVERAGE

B

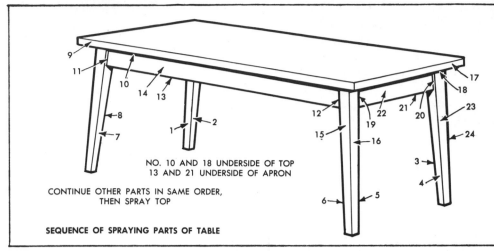

NO. 10 AND 18 UNDERSIDE OF TOP
13 AND 21 UNDERSIDE OF APRON

CONTINUE OTHER PARTS IN SAME ORDER,
THEN SPRAY TOP

SEQUENCE OF SPRAYING PARTS OF TABLE

than the legs. The inside of the legs is done first. For square legs, two sides of each can be sprayed from one position, rotating the turntable for each leg. For round legs, the inside of all the legs should be sprayed first; then each leg should be completed separately. Next, the edges of the table top are done, the underside of the extending top and the apron, and then the outside of the legs. The top should be done last. On cabinets and casework, where the inside is to be finished, this should be sprayed first, then the outside.

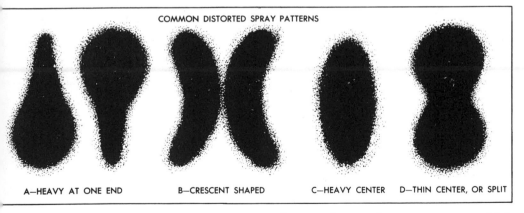

COMMON DISTORTED SPRAY PATTERNS

A—HEAVY AT ONE END   B—CRESCENT SHAPED   C—HEAVY CENTER   D—THIN CENTER, OR SPLIT

Partial clogging of the air cap will cause distorted spray patterns which are either heavy on the top or bottom, or sometimes are even crescent-shaped. A heavy center pattern may be due to a low setting on the spreader-adjustment valve, low atomizing pressure in a twin-jet cap, thick paint, too much fluid pressure (with pressure-feed guns), or an excess flow of liquid which is beyond the normal capacity of the air cap. A split or open-center spray pattern is caused by improper balance between air and fluid; it can be remedied by reducing the width of the spray pattern or increasing the fluid pressure. A fluttering spray is caused by air getting into the fluid line, which occurs when the cup becomes empty or the gun is tilted so that the fluid tube is only partly submerged. It can also be caused by a fluid tube which is loose and allows air to enter. On a suction-feed gun, jerky spraying can result from using too thick a liquid, a clogged vent hole in the lid, a loose coupling nut on the lid, or a loose needle packing at the fluid valve.

To clean the spray gun, the paint cup should be emptied, cleaned, and filled to one-quarter capacity with the correct solvent for the material you have been spraying. With the compressor turned off, the gun should be tipped, and the fluid tube should be allowed to drip a few seconds before the excess paint is wiped from the tube and the inside of the cap. The compressor may then be turned on and the solvent sprayed through the gun four or five times for a couple of seconds each time. Hold a cloth tightly against the nozzle, and pull the trigger a few times to force air inside the cup; the air will agitate the solvent within the cup and fluid tube. After the cup is removed, wipe the cap and outside of the gun with solvent. The trigger should be pulled to blow out any solvent remaining in the fluid tube. All paint residue from the threaded portions of both cup and cover should be removed. A caustic alkaline cleaner should not be used since this can damage aluminum parts.

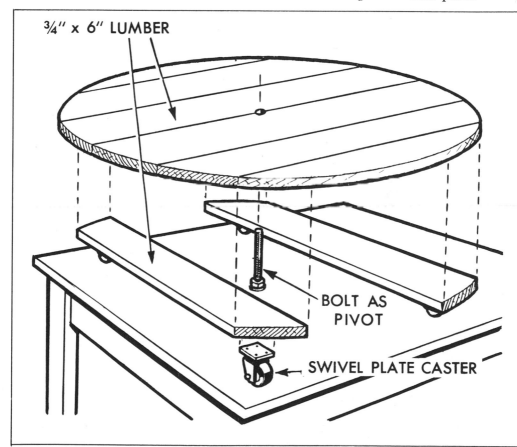

¾″ x 6″ LUMBER

BOLT AS PIVOT

SWIVEL PLATE CASTER

Spraying turntables, easily constructed out of inexpensive materials, are very helpful.

OTHER BASIC EQUIPMENT

Abrasives are used to remove old finishes, to prepare surfaces for new finishes, to act as a rub-down between finishing coats, and to polish.

Probably the most familiar abrasive tool is *coated abrasive*, or *sandpaper*, which is paper or cloth coated with abrasive particles. Originally, the abrasive grains of finishing papers were ground glass; later, sharp sand was used. Today, several different mineral grains are commonly used in making paper-backed abrasive sheets.

Flint paper is coated with particles of flint quartz, commonly called flint. While it is the least expensive abrasive paper, it is also the least effective. However, its low cost makes it popular for throw-away jobs, such as paint removal or the sanding of resinous wood, which soon clog even the most expensive abrasive papers.

Garnet paper is coated with an abrasive which comes from the same source as the semi-precious stone which bears that name. Red in color, the particles have a sharp, long-wearing, cutting edge. They are widely used in both professional and amateur wood finishing.

Aluminum oxide, unlike the above two abrasives, is not a natural mineral. This tough, long-wearing abrasive, made by fusing bauxite at very high temperatures, cuts both metal and wood.

Below: Samples of aluminum oxide sandpaper show different grades, open and closed coats.

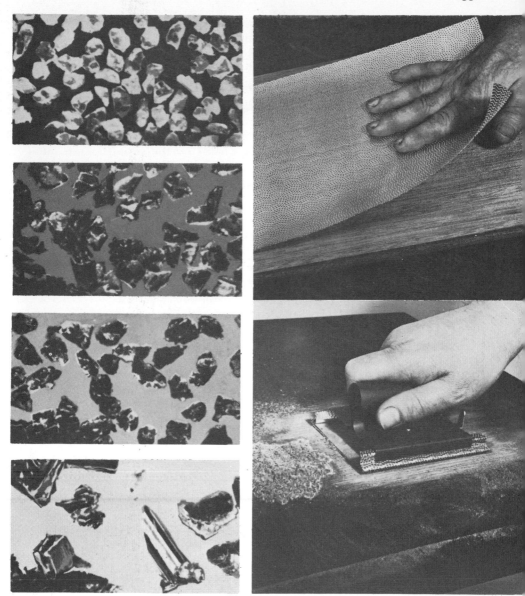

Top right: A sheet of metal abrasive. Metal abrasives are made by punching small, rough-edged holes in metal sheet. They are extremely long wearing, can be used in several commercial sanding blocks (*lower right*). *Above left:* Enlarged photos of mineral abrasives.

Silicon carbide, another artificial mineral, is a distant relative of the diamond. It is made by fusing silica sand with coke at very high temperature, and has a sharp, hard-cutting edge. This light gray abrasive also works well on almost any material, such as lacquers, plastics, and metals.

Coated abrasives are classified according to the size and distribution of the abrasive particles, or *grit*. Closed-coat papers are entirely covered with abrasive grains; while open-coat papers have only fifty to seventy per cent of the surface covered, leaving spaces between the grains. Closed-coat papers cut faster, but they are likely to become clogged when used on soft woods, paints, etc. Such jobs require an open-coat paper.

One reason why the shopper is often confused by the terms used to describe sandpaper is that today there are three entirely separate systems for classifying grit. The oldest is the *symbol scale*, which uses completely arbitrary symbols (such as 4, 3, 2, 1, 1/0, 2/0) to designate the size of the abrasive grains. This system has largely been replaced by the simpler mesh number system.

Abrasive particles are sorted by sifting them through a series of woven silk screens. The mesh number of a particular size grit (e.g., 16, 24, 50, 80, 100) refers to the actual number of openings per linear inch in the finest screen through which the particles can pass. Manufacturers now label abrasive papers with much broader and clearer texture classifications; e.g., "very fine," "fine," "medium," and "coarse." Since the mesh number accurately describes the size of the particles, it is the most reliable. The following table shows you the relationship between the three systems:

Texture	Mesh Number	Symbol
	400	10/0
	320	9/0
Very Fine	280	8/0
	240	7/0
	220	6/0
	180	5/0
Fine	150	4/0
	120	3/0
	100	2/0
Medium	80	1/0
	60	½
	50	1
Coarse	40	1½
	36	2
	30	2½
	24	3
Very Coarse	20	3½
	16	4
	12	4½

Backing to which the abrasive particles are bonded may be paper, cloth, a combination of paper and cloth, or even plastic. (One company is producing a Mylar-backed paper designed for model makers which is also handy in some refinishing jobs.)

Paper backing comes in four weights, with the lighter papers usually used for the finer grits. The lightest and most pliable paper backing, *A-grade*, is used with fine grits to make finishing papers. Medium-weight backings, *C-* and *D-grades*, are coated with slightly coarser grits to make cabinet papers. The heaviest paper backing, *E-grade*, is known as *roll stock*, and is usually used only for machine sanding.

Two common grades of cloth backing are *J-grade* and *X-grade*. J-grade, the lighter of the two, is used for hand sanding, and X-grade is generally used for power sanders. Most cloth and paper backings can be obtained in waterproof or wet-or-dry types for use in wet sanding.

Pumice stone is the favorite abrasive of the cabinetmaker for cutting down the final coats preparatory to rubbing down, or polishing; it is sometimes used instead of wet sanding with earlier coats. Rubbing the finishing coat smooths out small imperfections and removes dust specks. Pumice comes in four grades: "F," "FF," "FFF," and "FFFF," the last being the finest. *Rottenstone*, much finer than pumice, is used for the final rubbing operation. It is a polishing material, available in only one grade. Powdered abrasives are usually applied either with a felt pad or cloth.

Used for the same general purposes as sandpaper, *steel wool* commonly comes in six different grades. *No. 3* (coarse), *No. 2* (medium coarse), *No. 1* (medium), *No. 0* (fine), *No. 00* (very fine), and *No. 000* (super fine). The coarser grades are especially useful for removing old finishes where a scraper can't be used. Medium and fine grades often are used instead of powdered abrasives for rubbing finishing coats.

Wet sanding and rubbing with abrasive powders require the use of a *lubricant*. Water is the most common lubricant for between-coat abrasive operations because oil is hard to remove and will slow the drying of varnish. An exception to this is shellac, where rubbing should always be lubricated with oil. *Rubbing oils* are made by thinning light motor oil, paraffin oil, or crude petroleum with benzine; *polishing oils*, used in the final rubbing operation, are usually made from olive oil or lemon oil.

Special rubbing compounds must be used with lacquer, because it is a much harder finish. These compounds come in paste form and are graded acording to the size of the abrasive particles they contain; i.e., fine, medium, or coarse.

In addition to normal hand tools, power tools are especially helpful when finishing or refinishing a piece of furniture. With a well-equipped workshop, a hobbyist can even make a new arm or leg for a chair, duplicating the operations of the original craftsman.

Portable power sanders can save a lot of elbow grease. While the circular motion of a disk sander is likely to leave curved scratch patterns if not used carefully, it can be used to remove old finishes. The belt sander is even better for rough sanding, since the cutting action can follow the grain of the wood. The finishing, or orbital, sander is best of all for the final sanding before finishing.

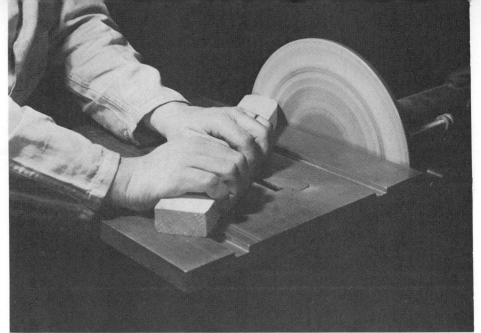

Preceding page: Drum sander attached to drill press does rough sanding but leaves marks. *Above:* Plate-backed abrasive disk attached to a circular saw makes a very useful sander, especially for end-grain jobs. *Below: The* "picking stick," easily made and very useful, can be still more useful—for delicate work—if a cloth is wrapped around sharpened end.

Several inexpensive items come in handy when removing old finishes. For instance, once you have softened the old finish with a remover, a *picking stick* is useful for cleaning carvings or turnings. To make this tool, sharpen one end of a ⅜-inch dowel and thin the other end to form a blade.

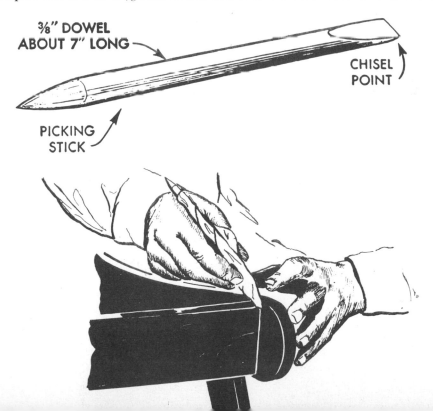

⅜" DOWEL ABOUT 7" LONG

CHISEL POINT

PICKING STICK

Another good tool for removing old paint from crevices is a common toothbrush. A putty knife with a rounded edge is the standard tool for lifting an old finish after it has been softened with remover.

On some rougher jobs, a torch with a fan tip can be used to soften the old finish before scraping it off with a scraper. However, unless used with a great deal of care, this technique can prove hazardous. It is not recommended for use on fine furniture.

II

Woods

GROWTH AND DEVELOPMENT

Although the finisher does not have the same interest in wood that the botanist has, he nevertheless must acquire some general knowledge in order to understand the characteristics of lumber and the methods of finishing the exposed surfaces when the material is used in a piece of furniture. The botanist primarily thinks of wood as a material which makes up the stem, or trunk, of certain large plants; therefore, his terminology describes the various characteristics of wood as a part of this living plant.

In botany, trees are divided into two general categories according to the method by which they bear seed. *Gymnosperms* are those whose ovules grow on the outer side of bracts (such as the cones of pine trees), and are fertilized by pollen carried by the wind; *angiosperms* are fertilized through the pistil of the flower, usually by means of pollen carried by insects, and their ovules are enclosed in a fruit. The botanical terms for the various cells, vessels, and ducts which make up the wood describe these structures according to their function in the life of the tree.

All common commercial woods are divided into two main classifications: *softwoods*, which are cut from conifers (cone-bearing trees), and *hardwoods*, which are cut from deciduous (flower-bearing) trees.

Although most "hardwoods" are harder than "softwoods," many so-called softwoods have a harder texture and physical structure than other woods which are designated as hardwoods. As an example, Southern Pine (in the United States) is a much harder wood than balsa; yet Southern Pine is classified as a softwood and balsa a hardwood. These classifications were established largely by means of custom and usage, but also from the physical structure and adaptabilities of the wood itself. However much such classifications in lumber grading and classifying may seem paradoxical to the novice, the beginner should not be as much concerned with these classifications as

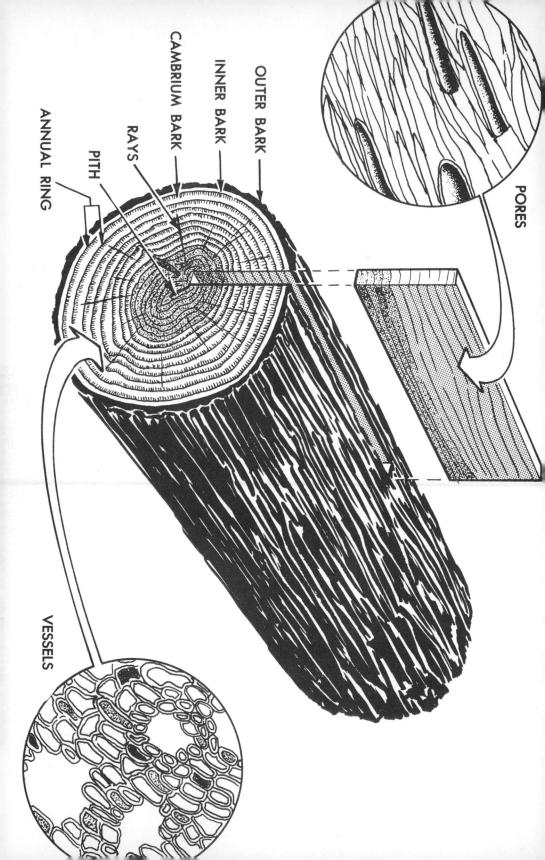

OUTER BARK

INNER BARK

CAMBRIUM BARK

RAYS

PITH

ANNUAL RING

PORES

VESSELS

with the methods used to produce a finish on the surface of the stock after it has been utilized as a raw material.

The trunk of a tree is made up of fibrous strands of elongated cells, each of which has a wall composed primarily of cellulose which gives the tree mechanical strength. The fibers of softwood trees are constructed so that they carry sap up the trunk of the tree. Hardwood trees have long sap vessels among the normal wood fibers which follow the line of growth. These vessels are strings of large-diameter, open-ended cells. When a log is cut into lumber and these cells are ruptured, they appear as minute cavities, or tiny grooves, in the surface of the lumber. These cavities are called *pores*.

In one sense, all hardwoods should be called *porous* woods because they have pores; softwoods are *non-porous* because they lack such pores. However, there is a great variation in the size of these pores in different woods. This is of special interest to the finisher since large-pored woods usually are filled in order to achieve a smooth finish. Therefore, for finishing purposes these woods are divided into two groups: *open-grain* woods (large-pored hardwoods such as oak and ash), which ordinarily need filling if a smooth finish is to be achieved; and *close-grain* woods (small-pored hardwoods, and all softwoods on which a filler is not ordinarily used). Other terms sometimes are used

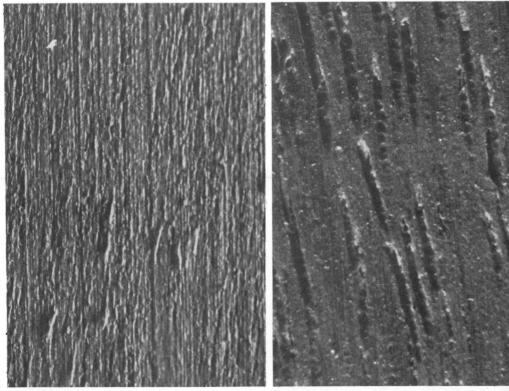

Left: Close-grained wood (highly magnified), which requires only a thin, liquid filler.
Right: Open-grained wood, enlarged to show large pores, usually requiring paste filler.

instead of open- or close-grain; for example, porous and non-porous, or coarse- and fine-grain. The chart which follows shows the characteristics of the most common woods:

HARDWOODS		SOFTWOODS
Open-Grain *	Close-Grain **	Close-Grain **
Ash	Apple	Basswood
Beech	Birch	Cedar
Butternut	Cherry	Cottonwood
Chestnut	Ebony (Africa-India)	Cypress
Elm	Maple	Fir
Mahogany	Pear	Gum
Oak		Pine
Walnut		Redwood

*   Requires paste filler
** Requires either a thin filler or none at all

In addition to the vertical wood fibers and vessels, there are also layers of cells which are horizontally arranged. These are called *medullary rays:* they extend from the inner bark toward the heart of the tree and conduct food inward and water outward. These rays, or flakes, are exposed on the surface of the board when oak or some of the other hardwoods are quarter-sawed from a log. There are a number of other structures in woods: these do not directly affect the finishing procedures and are not, therefore, pertinent to the interests of the finisher.

Staining emphasizes the grain of a wood. Refinishers say it "gives wood more character."

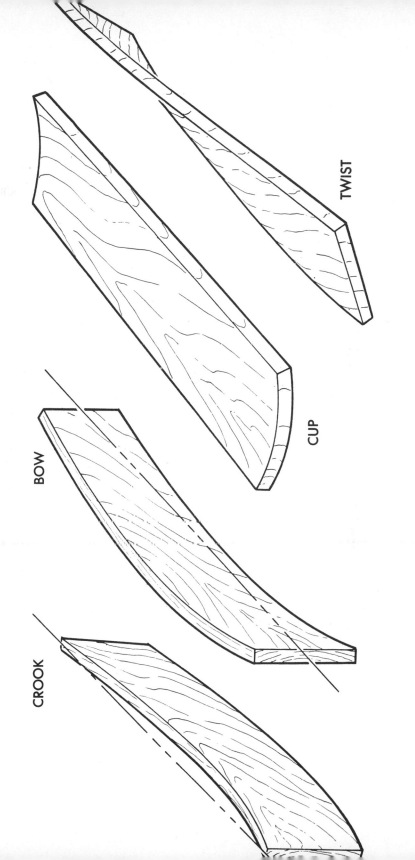

CROOK

BOW

CUP

TWIST

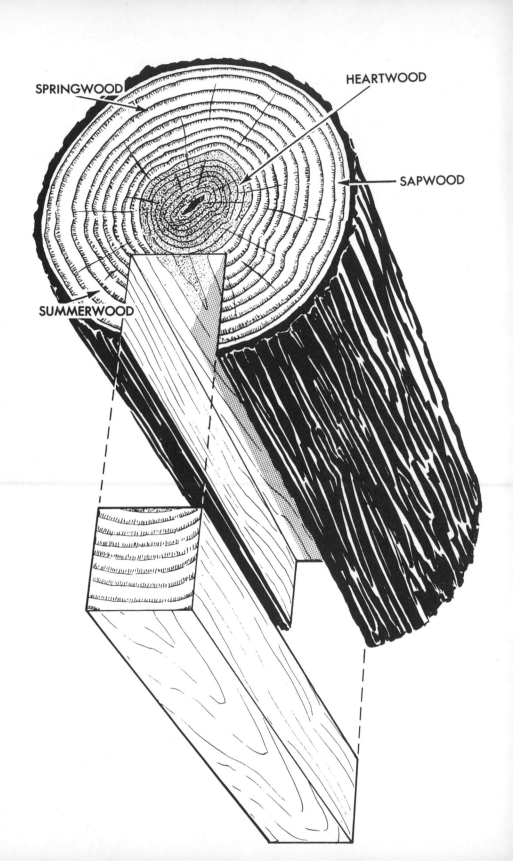

SPRINGWOOD

HEARTWOOD

SAPWOOD

SUMMERWOOD

The grain pattern found in any piece of lumber is determined by the size, quality, and arrangement of its cells, and by the method used to cut the lumber from the log. In tree growth, layer after layer of new cells are added just beneath the inner cambium bark (a soft formation tissue) which gives rise to these new cells. While the cells of any one species of trees bear a basic resemblance to the cells of other species, nevertheless, there is a certain amount of variation between the different layers of cells in a tree which grows in a temperate climate, due to its seasonal growth cycle.

The new wood, which lies just beneath the bark, is called *sapwood*. As the name implies, it is this part which is most active in carrying the sap up the trunk of the tree. The *heartwood*, which lies under the sapwood, is denser and it becomes less and less active as the tree ages. Each spring many layers of large thin-walled cells are formed in the trunks of deciduous trees, in order to carry the extra sap necessary to produce new foliage. Once the new leaves have been produced, the growth rate slows. The cells added during this period are not only smaller, but they also have thicker walls. Thus, *summerwood*, which grows slowly, is dense and darker in color than *springwood*, which grows rapidly. This variation is shown in the familiar annual rings in any cross section of a log; when the log is cut into lumber, this pattern is known as the *grain* of the lumber.

Summerwood

CUTS, GRAINS AND FIGURES

There are a number of common *grain patterns*. If the growth rings are wide and conspicuous, the wood is referred to as a *coarse-grained* wood. This same term is often used to describe wood having large pores, generally because this pattern is usually found in rapidly growing trees with large cells. Wood which has narrower, less conspicuous rings is called *fine-* or *close-grained*. Again, these terms are also used to describe small-pored woods.

When the summerwood is particularly conspicuous and the annual rings are therefore irregular in width, the wood is said to have an *uneven* grain. The opposite of this, *even grain,* is a term applied to wood with little contrast in its annual rings. The term *straight-grained* means that the wood fibers run almost parallel to the main axis of the log. If the fibers take a spiral course around the axis of the tree, the wood is said to have a *spiral* grain.

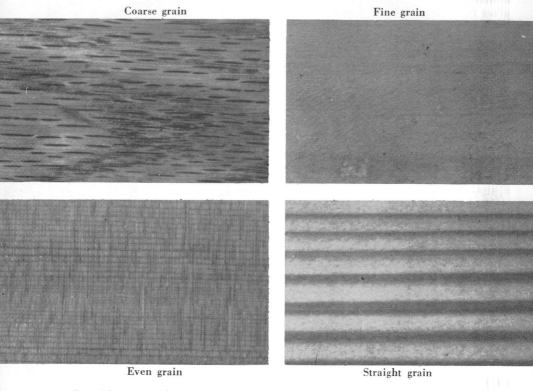

Coarse grain

Fine grain

Even grain

Straight grain

In addition to the grain patterns mentioned above, there are terms which describe the grains brought about by the way a piece of lumber is cut from the log. When the plane of the cut forms a radius to the annual rings, the lumber is said to be *quarter-sawed*; it then shows a *vertical* grain. *Plain-sawed* lumber is cut on a tangent to the growth rings and consequently is called *flat-grained*. When wood is not cut parallel to the fibers of a straight-grained log, the result is *diagonal* grain.

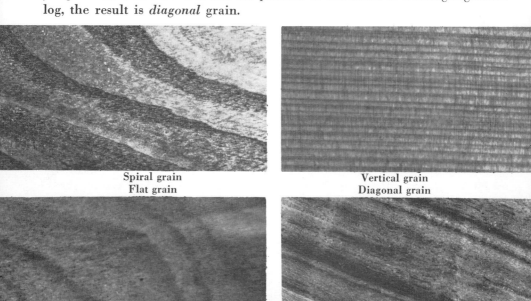

Spiral grain
Flat grain

Vertical grain
Diagonal grain

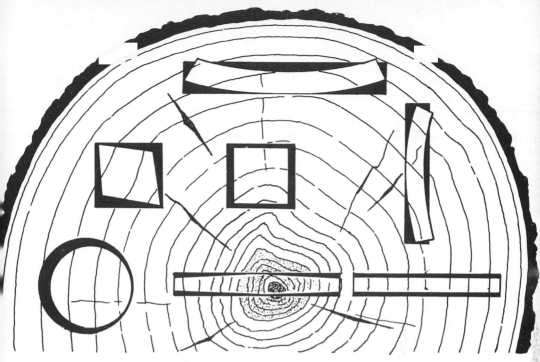

Above: Diagram shows several different ways boards are cut from timber, and their common warping tendencies. *Below:* End and side views of grains of quarter- and plain-sawed wood.

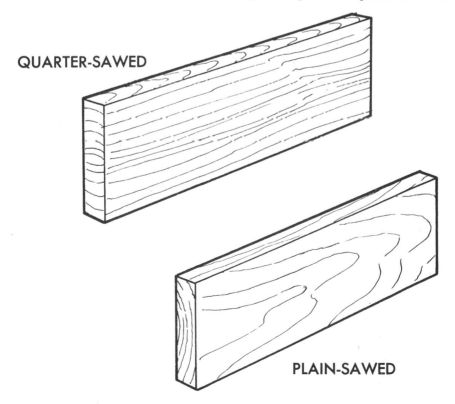

QUARTER-SAWED

PLAIN-SAWED

Some of the most beautiful grain patterns are found in *veneers*. A furniture *veneer* is a very thin sheet of superior wood which is glued to a less expensive "backing" wood, or *core*. These thin sheets are produced by slicing around the log, or by cutting through it with a saw. They can be cut at almost any angle and from any portion of the log. The cheaper veneers used in plywood are usually produced on large veneer lathes by a rotary cutting process. Veneering is a very old process, one which is still regarded as the most efficient means of fully utilizing the decorative beauty and color of an expensive wood. If it were not for veneers, some of the furniture woods would be priced beyond the reach of most people, and it would be impossible to make use of many of the beautiful grain patterns which are available only in rotary and saw-cut veneers.

There are several special figures or patterns; for example, in quarter-sawed oak and sycamore the medullary rays are often large and prominent, forming a figure which is called a *silver grain.*

Although comparatively rare, plain-sawed lumber may show a *blister figure* grain, produced by an uneven contour of the annual rings. This is especially prized in maple, mahogany, and walnut, although the latter is rare. A *quilted figure* grain is one which resembles a blister figure but it usually covers a much larger area. It is generally present in wood found below the larger limbs of leaning trees where pressure has caused the fibers to form corrugations in the grain.

A *wavy figure* grain pattern occurs most frequently in the wood at the base of the tree where the roots join the trunk, or immediately below the crotch where the limb extends from the trunk. The *fiddle-back figure* is found principally in maple and mahogany. In maple, this very fine, wavy figure is popular for violin backs; hence the name. When wood fibers extend irregularly in short wavy configurations and the grain of the wood is twisted or interwoven, it forms a *mottle figure*. This is frequently found in quarter-sawed lumber, especially in walnut-butt veneers.

A *burl* is a wart-like, abnormal growth on the outside layer of a tree trunk, usually the result of an injury to the tree. It contains dark piths of buds which never developed, and distorted, irregular fibers which run in no particular direction. Although burls may occur in any kind of tree, the burls of walnut, maple, cherry, ash, and birch are the most desirable, and are used extensively in fine furniture veneers.

The *snail figure*, which somewhat resembles a burl, comes from the trunk and stump of the tree, rather than from the burl formation. It is usually found only in Black Walnut.

In a *bird's-eye figure* the "eyes" are conical indentations or tiny knots in the grain, which usually extend from near the center of the log to the outside layer and are sometimes discernible even in the bark. In some trees, however, these eyes extend in from the outer portion of the log only a few inches. This figure is most often found in a few Sugar Maple trees, but also occurs in Soft Maple, White Ash, Yellow Birch, and some pines.

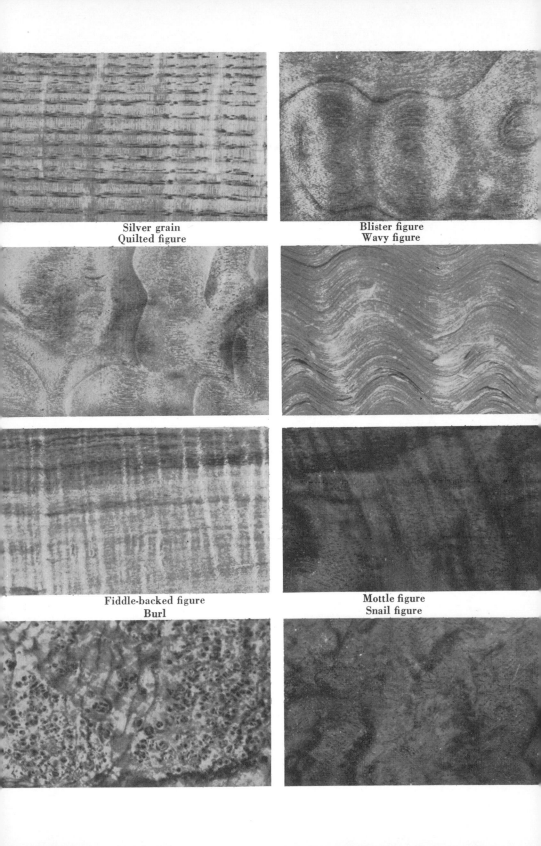

Silver grain
Quilted figure

Blister figure
Wavy figure

Fiddle-backed figure
Burl

Mottle figure
Snail figure

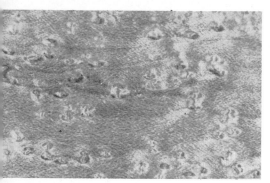

Above: Bird's-eye figure shown in milled lumber (*left*) and in unmilled chunks (*right*).

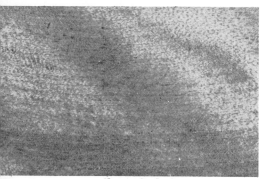

Above: Curly figure
Below: Crotch figure

Above: Swirl figure
Below: Feather crotch figure

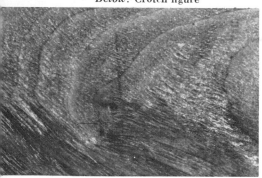

The *curly figure* is found in wood having fibers which form waves of undulations, which generally surround knots in the trunk. This figure is quite common in many hardwoods, but is also found, more rarely, in softwoods. A mottled and burl-like *swirl figure* is found in veneer which has been cut from a barrel-shaped bulge in a log, such as those found in many hardwoods. Where large limbs join the trunk or at the main forks of larger limbs, a *crotch figure* is produced. It is usually Y-shaped, and is rather common. A *feather-crotch figure*, which is also sometimes referred to as a *flame grain*, is a figure in which the fibers always fan out, thus giving the appearance of a cluster of feathers.

POPULAR FURNITURE WOODS

The foregoing outlined the various common characteristics used to differentiate one wood from another in order to clarify the brief descriptions of the most common furniture woods. Descriptions of these woods follow:

Walnut—This has always been a very popular furniture wood because of its coloring and the variety of beautiful figures which may be found in it. The color of walnut varies from a light gray-brown to a dark purplish-brown. Black Walnut (the American variety) takes its name from the color of the nut shells rather than the color of the wood. Almost every finish known has been used on walnut at one time or another.

Walnut is between oak and mahogany in hardness. This makes it relatively easy to work with, but strong enough to be used in slender structural elements. The wood is strong and uniform in texture. It can easily be worked on with hand and power tools. The crotches, burls, and stumps produce figured and mottled grain patterns which are beautiful; these are frequently found in veneers of high quality. Walnut can be satisfactorily glued; it polishes exceptionally well, holds its shape and, after proper seasoning, shrinks or swells very little. Although highly prized by all earlier cabinet-makers, walnut was especially popular during the Civil War period when it was used for elaborately carved, darkly stained chests, chairs, and tables. Most contemporary or modern furniture employs an oil finish of a lighter color, which emphasizes the graining of the wood.

Walnut and other hardwoods which are grown in the uplands are quite different from woods which come from the lowlands. The adversity of the upland environment slows the growth of the tree, producing a more distinctive, finer wood grain. Wood from the same species which has been grown in the lowlands is coarser in texture, is of a color which tends toward a lighter shade, and has less attractive graining. The finest American antique walnut pieces were made from wood which was cut from virgin timber grown in the Appalachian Mountains or in the uplands of the New England states.

Mahogany—This wood also has a great variety of grain figures. It is easy to cut or carve and, although softer than many other hardwoods, it has an excellent strength-to-weight ratio. Some of the wider boards used in furniture construction come from the huge trunk of the mahogany tree.

Most people think that mahogany is a wood that is naturally red due to the extreme popularity of the familiar red finish introduced in the eighteenth century by Thomas Chippendale and by the cabinetmakers who were his contemporaries. Natural mahogany, however, is actually a light, cherry brown. Its consistently fine quality and even grain make slicing possible and its open grain is advantageous for gluing, making mahogany especially suitable for use as a veneer over secondary woods.

Black Cherry—The popularity of this wood in America can be traced all the way back to the late seventeenth century. The mention of cherry furniture to most homemakers automatically recalls Colonial breakfronts, Federal chairs, and Early American spool beds.

The cherry used for furniture is Wild Black Cherry, the color of which varies from the white of the sapwood to the dark amber of aged heartwood. Although this is a close-grained wood with markings which are relatively inconspicuous and undramatic when it has been flat-sawed, cherry is particularly suitable for conservative designs. When quarter-sawed, the wood sometimes shows a *flaky* figure, and highly figured veneers are often found in selected cherry.

Maple—Reproductions of Early American pieces are often stained various shades of reddish-brown; these are the modern equivalent of many early maple pieces, which were finished with a thin red paint. Authentic Early American maple pieces were also finished in a soft yellow-brown.

Most furniture stock is cut from the Sugar Maple; it is usually straight-grained with a color ranging from pinkish-white (sapwood) to dark red-brown (heartwood). Some pieces of solid stock show a bird's-eye figure or a curly grain, but these are usually graded and sold as violin stock. Because maple is exceptionally close-grained with almost invisible pores, it needs no filling, but it is a little more difficult to glue with animal glues than woods which are more porous. Modern adhesives, however, have overcome this difficulty for the most part.

Birch—The wood used in furniture comes from either the yellow birch or sweet birch tree. The latter (sometimes called Black Birch) was more popular in Colonial times. Because of its dark, reddish-brown color, it was also called "mountain mahogany." Yellow birch, on the other hand, is a warm light brown with a great variety of figures. This makes it a highly desirable material for furniture veneers.

Oak—Oak has been used for furniture since early Greek times. It went out of fashion toward the end of the seventeenth century when "more refined" furniture styles became popular; however, it regained popularity during the Victorian period. Unfortunately, it was often used by designers who failed to take advantage of its best points, but it now finds quite wide use in contemporary furniture construction.

Oak is open-grained, hard, and very strong. Its colors range from the light yellow of White Oak to the reddish amber of the Red Oak. Since the wood has a grain which is distinctly open, unusual effects can be obtained simply by varying the color of the filler used. However, many period finishes, for example, Mission and Jacobean, required that the pores be left open.

III

From Start to Finish

REMOVING THE OLD

Although removing the old finish is one of the messiest parts of any refinishing operation, it can also be one of the most rewarding. A real thrill may be found in the discovery of a beautiful wood which has been hidden for years under old coats of paint, varnish, and dirt. With the new paint and varnish removers, which usually are called simply *varnish removers* by professional finishers, no special skill or back-breaking labor is involved. However, the job *does* require patience and painstaking care. Any of three common methods of removing paint can be used when stripping an old piece of furniture; i.e., mechanical, heat, or chemical.

MECHANICAL REMOVAL

Simple removal of the old finish by sanding or scraping, without the aid of chemicals or heat, is best suited to pieces with large, flat surfaces which have few decorative carvings, turnings, or moldings. It is wise, however, to bear in mind that this method removes the old finish and a thin layer of the old wood itself, along with the aged-in beauty which is known to collectors as the *patina*, or age color. Often the antique character of a worn, marked surface and the patina are appealing characteristics which a finisher may wish to preserve under a new transparent finish. If this is the case, it is well to rely on chemical paint and varnish removers. But when a piece requires a great deal of patching and repair which is to be masked with an opaque finish, one of the easiest ways of removing the old finish is by means of a power sander. Even though you are contemplating the use of transparent finish, it is often preferable to remove signs of wear by sanding or scraping.

Nonetheless, simple mechanical removal of the old finish has certain advantages. For one thing, it isn't as messy. Ventilation and temperature are not important when one takes down (or strips) a simple, square chest by using a belt sander. It is true that dust once caused a problem, but many of today's belt sanders have an accessory dust collector which eliminates this worry. A disk sander may be used for the rough sanding but, unless the finisher switches to straight-line, belt sanding or hand sanding before he reaches the wood itself, the disk sander's rotary action may leave scars on the surface.

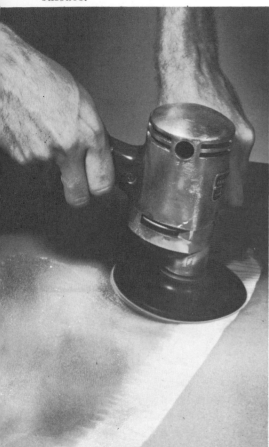 

Left: Disk sanders are used to remove old finishes but circular action scratches wood. *Right:* Better for refinishing are belt sanders, which move in the direction of the grain.

The correct use of a cabinet scraper is definitely an art, and in the hands of an enthusiastic but unskilled amateur a hooked scraper can cause irreparable damage. When used correctly, a hooked cabinet scraper removes a thin layer of wood along with the finish. However, the amateur may find it difficult to keep an even surface and to avoid gouging the wood.

As a general rule for most refinishing jobs, it is best to use judicious sanding and scraping to supplement chemical removal.

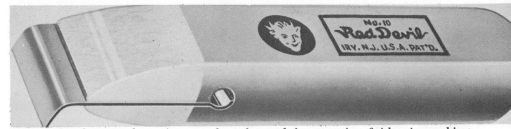

The simplest but not the easiest nor the safest tool for removing finishes is a cabinet scraper, which can gouge deeply. *Above:* A hooked scraper. *Below:* A double-edged scraper.

The method of removing the finish by heat can be rated somewhere between simply sanding off the old finish and using a varnish remover. Instead of using chemicals, a torch equipped with a fan tip which spreads the flame is moved slowly over the old finish until it begins to soften. A warning is needed here, however, for extreme care must be taken in order to avoid a fire hazard. Once the old finish has been softened, it can be removed with a scraper, putty knife, or wire brush.

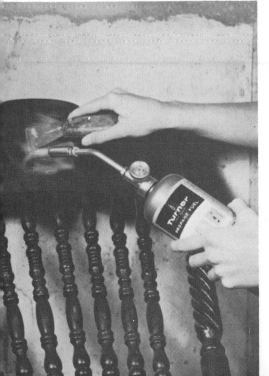

A torch is very useful, but scorching is a constant hazard. Torches should not be used on fine furniture. *Left* and *above:* Use with putty knife on flats, with brush on turnings.

Electric finish removers work on this same principle, providing heat without flame, which reduces the danger of scorching the wood. Like sanding, this method is most suitable for removing the old finish from a piece which is to receive a new opaque finish.

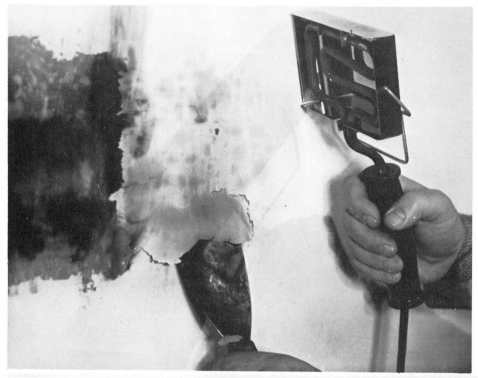

Removing paint with an electric heater is much like using an open-flame torch. Both work quite fast but often scorch wood. Both are best used if an opaque finish will be applied.

CHEMICAL REMOVERS

The standard method of removing an old finish is by use of chemicals, which soften the old finish and break the bond with the wood, so that the resulting sludge can be stripped off with a putty knife, or washed off with clean water if one of the new "wash-off" removers has been used.

There are many recipes for home-made removers, but these can not match the speed, efficiency, and safety of the latest commercial removers. The original finish on many antiques was shellac or some other spirit varnish, and denatured alcohol will soften and aid in removing such finishes. Moreover, this method is somewhat cheaper than using commercial removers. However, since the possibility exists that the piece has been refinished more recently with a clear finish that can not be removed with alcohol, it is preferable to use a commercial varnish remover which will do both jobs equally well.

Another method, which is widely used by restorers of valuable antiques, is that of removing the old finish simply by rubbing it off with pads of steel wool charged with a creamy paste, or *slurry*, of linseed oil and fine pumice. Hard-felt rubbing pads are sometimes substituted for steel wool, and rubbing oil or lemon oil often is substituted for linseed oil. This procedure is rather tedious to carry out, and the piece must be cleaned frequently and examined closely in order to keep check on the progress.

Commercial paint and varnish removers are available in three forms: liquid, semi-paste, and paste. A remover must remain on the surface for some time—at least ten or fifteen minutes—in order to penetrate the old finish. For this reason, the liquid form doesn't work well on vertical surfaces. However, it is usually possible to turn small pieces on their side so that you are always working on a horizontal surface, preventing the liquid remover from running off the piece. These penetrating solvents (which actually soften the finish) evaporate rapidly; therefore, many paint removers have a wax base which forms a surface skin to slow down evaporation. Wax-free removers act slightly slower, but they are preferable in many respects. They simplify the clean-up procedure, which otherwise consists of removing any wax which remains on the surface after the old finish has been removed with a cleaning agent. If the wax is not removed, it will slow down the drying process in the new finish and sometimes may even cause peeling. Wax-free removers make such an operation unnecessary.

Many removers require a special water or solvent rinse after the finish has been removed in order to neutralize their action. Other "no-rinse" types are self-neutralizing and require no special operation to stop the action of the remover. Either solvent or water rinses may raise the grain of the wood; water rinses also act on water-sensitive glues by loosening joints. You can minimize such dangers by being especially careful when rinsing and by using no more neutralizer than is absolutely necessary.

The flammability (or inflammability) of a remover is determined by the volatile solvents it contains: most flammable removers contain *benzol*, a solvent which is not only flammable but also highly toxic when inhaled over a prolonged period of time. Non-flammable removers are relatively new; they are usually more expensive because they contain volatile ingredients which serve to smother flames rather than encourage them. In addition to the flammability of the removers themselves, it is necessary to take into consideration the interaction of the rinses and the solvent rinse-removers because the fire hazard is doubled when a flammable solvent rinse is used with a flammable remover.

Stripping a piece of furniture is a job which requires careful preparation. It is easiest when performed outside the house. If this is impossible because of the weather or for some other reason, the next most logical place is a basement which has a concrete floor. If you live in an apartment, however, and are forced to do the job on a tile or wood floor, several precautions should be taken. Strong solvents in removers can not tell the difference between the old finish and your shiny new kitchen tile, and they go to work on whatever they touch without preference. The safeguard of a couple of layers of newspapers only gives you a false sense of security, for removers are not nearly as docile as finishing materials are. They are designed to penetrate a surface, whether this be an old finish or an old newspaper. It is preferable to cut a few corrugated boxes apart and spread them over the floor in order to form a flat base at least two feet larger than the longest dimension of the piece which you are refinishing. This should be covered by at least half a dozen layers of newspaper. If you work carefully and confine all activity to this area, your floor is reasonably safe.

Any removers may irritate the skin and, in some instances, damage clothing; therefore, rubber gloves should be worn for the entire job. Any remover which accidentally gets on the skin or clothing should be washed off immediately.

When working with paint removers, it is important to protect both the skin and whatever surfaces are nearby. Spread several layers of newspaper under work, wear rubber gloves.

Adequate ventilation is especially important when you are working with flammable removers. The fumes from even non-flammable removers are toxic if you inhale them for an extended period of time. Note closely any warnings on containers, and during any refinishing job always give consideration to proper ventilation. Ideally, a ventilating fan should be installed in one of the windows of your basement. If you are an apartment dweller, the kitchen is probably the next best working area, especially if it has a ventilating fan. However, even if you have adequate ventilation, it is a good idea to take a break every half hour or so by going outdoors or into another room.

Temperature, both that of the air and that of the remover, is also important. When you strip off a finish outside in the sunlight, you'll find that the action will be slower because the volatile solvents "flash off" more quickly. On the other hand, if you are working in a chilly basement during the winter, you may have to warm the remover slightly by setting the can in warm water to speed the action. *Never* put it over an open flame. In warm weather, when the remover has been thinned by the heat, you can thicken it for use on vertical surfaces by chilling it in the refrigerator for a few minutes.

Work on one small section at a time—one which has a maximum area of one-and-a-half or two square feet. Since the remover works best on a horizontal surface, the piece should be turned on its side when you are working on the sides. Use an old brush when applying remover, making it flow in one direction only by using as few strokes as possible. Be liberal with the remover, for a coat which is too thin may necessitate a second application.

Apply remover liberally to a limited area, so that it is completely ready all at once.

The trick in stripping is to know when the remover has penetrated sufficiently. This point of sufficient penetration varies somewhat for different finishes, depending on whether you are using the same brand of remover, are working with the same number of finish coats, or at the same temperature. Opaque finishes usually wrinkle when the remover has penetrated the film and broken the bond, while clear finishes tend to form a thick sludge at the point where the remover has penetrated the film. The sludge should be

Left: After applying remover, test about ten minutes after wrinkles first show. *Right:* If all paint is loose down to the wood, then remove sludge with round-cornered putty knife.

broken the bond, while clear finishes tend to form a thick sludge at the point where the remover has penetrated the film. The sludge should be scraped off after the remover has penetrated completely, but before it has begun to dry. About five or ten minutes after the first wrinkling or sludging appears, test a small portion by lifting it with a broad putty knife. If the penetration is not complete, another test should be made in a few more minutes. On a piece covered with many layers of a finish such as paint or enamel, you will sometimes find that you can lift the various layers, which are separate films of the several coats. When this happens, it is better to remove the old finish layer by layer, applying fresh remover over the successive coats until you at last reach the bare wood.

Lifting tools should have even, dull blades. A wedge-shaped wooden block often works well.

The lifting tool (whether it be putty knife, scraper, or simply a block of wood with a wedge-shaped end) should have an even, dull blade which has rounded corners. If your putty knife has sharp corners, round them with a file to prevent gouging the wood with them. Burlap or steel wool bound with a string should be used to remove the sludge from turnings. Ornamental grooves and carvings can be cleaned with a picking stick, a fine steel brush, or a wooden meat skewer with a piece of steel wool fastened around the tip. A common toothbrush may be used, but the plastic handle or bristle is likely to soften if it comes into contact with the remover.

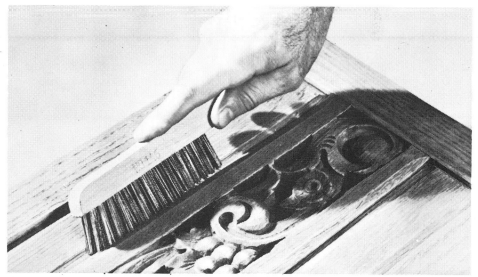

Steel-bristled brushes will clean grooves well but may scratch wood softened by remover.

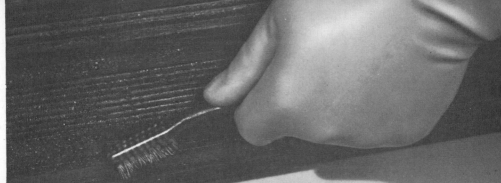

Top: Toothbrush will clean grooves and carvings, although remover may soften bristles and handle. *Above left:* Picking stick (see page 37) is another good tool for cleaning grooves. *Right:* A meat skewer tipped with steel wool works quite like a picking stick, cleans ornamental carvings without scratching. Though tedious this sort of cleaning is extremely important in refinishing. *Below:* Turnings, which could not be cleaned with most tools, should be rubbed with burlap.

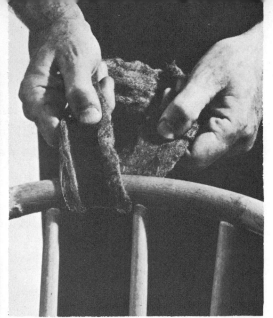

Left: After the sludge has been removed by putty knife (or another tool) the wood should be wiped by fine steel wool soaked with paint remover. On difficult turnings, as shown *top right,* tape can often be used to back the steel wool. On smaller turnings or grooved turnings (*above*), string can be entwined with the steel wool, thus increasing its strength and workability. *Below:* In slots or grooves too small for putty knives yet too large for picking sticks, molding tools may work well.

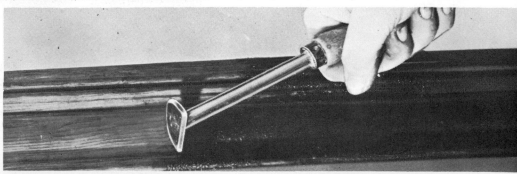

One absolutely sure way to avoid scratches is to wipe off the paint sludge with fine steel wool or a rough cloth which has been dipped in remover. This is slower and messier, but it is safe, especially for choice antiques where the finisher may wish to preserve that valued patina.

When all of the old finish has been removed, wash the entire piece with a cloth that has been saturated with a recommended neutralizer. All removers, of course, do not require the use of a neutralizer; when water is used for rinsing, it should be used sparingly to prevent raising the grain or discoloring the wood. When using no-rinse removers, all surfaces should be cleaned with a piece of fine steel wool which has been dipped into the remover. The piece should then be wiped with a cloth. If these instructions are contradicted by a particular manufacturer's, the latter's should be followed.

Above: Fine steel wool will remove a softened finish, avoids danger of scratching wood.
Below: After using "no-rinse" remover, take off all finish, then wipe with clean cloth.

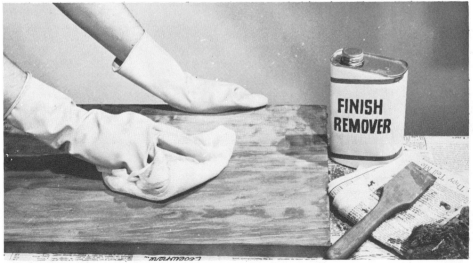

Remember that every bit of the old finish and remover must be taken off. Turpentine or alcohol can be used to remove wax. When applying the remover, be sure that it doesn't spatter or run into areas which have not yet been treated. In the case of wash-type removers, the depth of penetration is largely determined by the time between application and neutralizing, or wash-off. If drops or spatters aren't removed in time, they will leave stains in the wood which will require bleaching; therefore, you should immediately remove runs or drops with denatured alcohol or water to prevent staining.

After removing the old finish, the piece should be allowed to dry thoroughly for a period of at least twenty-four hours, or else the hardening of new finishes which have been applied over a surface on which remover has been used may be slowed down. Remember to take this into consideration when applying the different coats of the new finish. Make sure each coat is dry before the next one is applied.

WHEN TO REPAIR

When every trace of the old finish has been removed and all dents, scratches, and loose joints have been repaired, the schedule for applying a new finish is ordinarily much the same as that for unfinished or new wood. If a power sander was used to remove all the traces of the old finish, the surface should ordinarily be treated as new wood. However, in sanding or scraping off an old finish it is difficult to stop short of removing those desirable marks of age and use which are so highly prized by antiquarians and experienced antique collectors. On the other hand, chemical removers act on the old finish only and help to preserve this patina. Light, careful sanding smooths the old surface, and spot bleaching can be used as a last resort to remove unsightly discoloration. If the color of the wood itself is to be lightened, surface bleaching is needed, but this should be undertaken with caution. Naturally, any operations which involve the color of the wood or removal of surface discoloration are unnecessary if an opaque finish is to be used.

Before sanding is begun, the piece must be examined closely for surface defects. If cracks and scratches are too deep to be sanded away, or concealed with a filler, they must be filled with plastic wood of a color which will match the finish to be applied. Any exposed nail or screw holes should be masked with the same material. The piece should be checked for loose joints; if any are found, they must be cleaned and reglued before sanding. Some restorers completely dismantle very fine pieces which have defective joints, and clean and reglue them before refinishing.

Of the two main reasons for making all such repairs before sanding or finishing, the most obvious is that operations necessary to the repair may damage the surface. The other reason is to assure that all surfaces, including those portions which need repair, get the same treatment in operations such as sanding, filling, and staining.

SANDING

One of the most important operations in any finishing schedule is smoothing the surface of the wood before finishing. Experienced finishers and restorers are agreed that the finish can never be better than the surface over which it was applied. If the sanding schedule is rushed with the expectation that the new finish will conceal any shortcuts, the truth of the matter will soon be discovered. A professional finish applied to a fine piece is the craftsman's hallmark, and he will go to any lengths to achieve it. By taking the time to do a good job of sanding and by using correct procedures and the correct grades of abrasives, even the amateur can achieve a finish which will get a nod of approval from the pros.

Sanding may be done by hand or with any of a wide variety of power sanders. A portable belt sander is the most useful type for all-around work. The vibrator-type pad sander offers the cheapest power device, and is quite efficient when used with fine abrasives. Larger, oscillating, motor-driven, pad sanders of the straight-line and orbital types (these terms refer to the motion of the pad) are excellent for fine sanding, polishing, and rubbing operations. In both power and hand sanding, it is usually the practice to work with the grain. At points where two pieces of wood join, with the grain running in different directions, as in matched veneers, one part should be covered with tape while the other is sanded, then the sanded piece should be masked while the second piece is smoothed.

A portable power sander, especially a small belt sander, may mar the surface very easily if it is not properly used. Hold it so that the shoe rides flat on the surface because any tipping will cause the edge to dig in. Be sure to go over the surface evenly. The fast-cutting action of a power sander will produce low spots if it is not uniformly moved over the whole surface. All the precautions outlined for hand sanding are doubly important when a power sander is being used. When power sanding, you normally begin with the medium grits and go to the fine.

If for lack of a power sander all sanding must be performed by hand, selection of the proper abrasive and use of it in the correct manner will cut down the amount of elbow grease required. As a general rule, one of the fast-cutting coarse grits is used at the start; this is followed with a medium grit, and the smoothing is finished with fine and extra-fine grits. In refinishing a surface which is in good condition, the use of a coarse grit is often omitted. However, there are few definite rules within this general procedure. Different woods require different grits, and the same wood may even need different grits for different purposes. A little experience in working with sandpaper will give you a good idea of the capabilities of each grit and will aid in deciding which to use for a particular job.

To obtain a smooth and uniform action on a flat surface, with any abrasive paper the paper must be backed with a block of soft wood, although some finishers prefer hard-felt pads. Some commercial sanding blocks are

Several power sanders offer the advantage of being not merely portable, but changeable. With a flick of a switch this straight-line sander (*above*) changes to orbital (*below*).

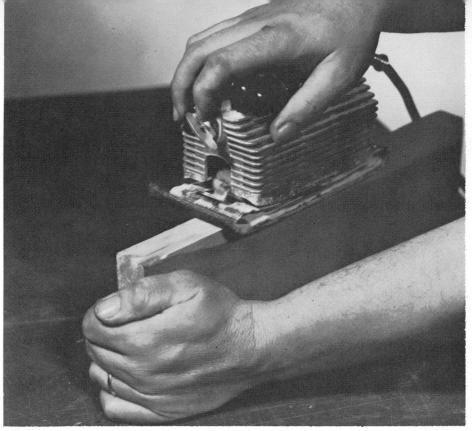

Above: This little sander's reciprocating action makes possible sanding with wood grains.
Below: Dust-collecting attachment connects to vacuum cleaner, keeps work and air clean.

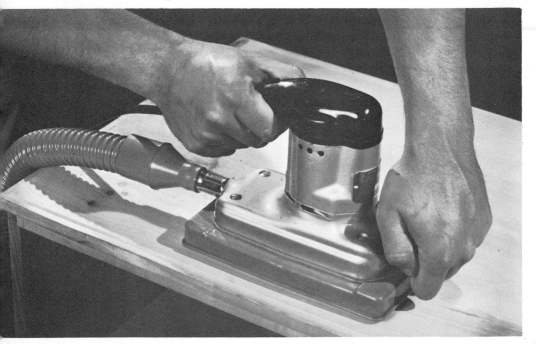

prepared with cloth-backed rolls; these are especially handy for working in corners, on rounded edges, or on wide moldings. A rubber sanding block is ideal for sanding curves with a long radius. An ordinary wood block without a pad is useful when cutting down ridges and other irregularities: the rigid backing causes the abrasive to cut very fast, with a leveling action on the whole area being sanded. However, there is some danger of gouging when one works with an unpadded block. When fitted with a thin felt pad, this desirable leveling action is somewhat reduced, but the danger of leaving deep scratches in the wood is lessened.

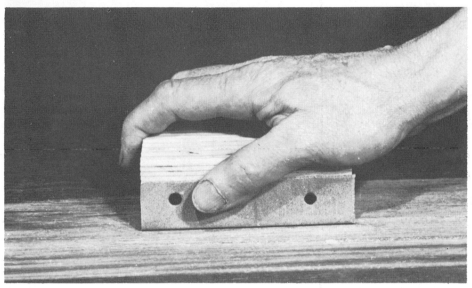

Above: The fastest sanding block has no padding, but has a tendency to gouge and scrape. *Below:* If a thin felt pad is inserted between the block and the paper, sanding is safer.

The trick which produces a true, flat surface when hand sanding is the use of uniform strokes and even pressure. If the craftsman places the work in front of him and strokes from side to side as far as he can reach in both directions, the ends of these strokes are likely to curve across the grain, and the pressure here will fall off. Experienced finishers use short, even strokes and move along the length of the work, overlapping on every stroke. When possible, the workman should sand away from himself, rather than from side to side. This technique will produce a surface which is acceptably flat, even on large pieces.

When sanding to an edge, the sanding block should not extend beyond the edge for more than about one-fourth of its length on each stroke; otherwise, the corner will tend to round over. All edges should be very slightly rounded (or softened, as cabinetmakers say) to hold the finish. However, this should be done only after a square edge has been produced by means of proper sanding.

When sanding to an edge, don't let the block extend more than one-fourth of its length.

On many old pieces, the finisher finds it necessary to sand molded shapes. An easy way of doing this is by making a special sanding block which has one edge shaped in reverse relief to the molding. A block such as this can be made with hand tools and, if care is taken to bring the shape to exact reverse relief, the molding can be cleaned without altering its shape appreciably. Or a number of pieces of thin stock (veneer is best) may be cut in handy sanding-block size. They are stacked, and one-quarter-inch slots are formed at the center by drilling adjacent holes and then removing the waste with a chisel. The pieces may be held together loosely with a quarter-inch stove bolt, and the block should then be set on the molding in such a way that it will take the shape of the molding. After the bolt is tightened and fine sandpaper has been wrapped around the edge, the block is complete.

Rough sanding is not always necessary when refinishing, but it levels ridges and removes other minor surface imperfections. Any of the coarser grades of abrasive papers can be used for this operation. When working with coarse, open-grained woods (such as chestnut, oak, or ash), a necessary exception to the rule about always sanding with the grain is made. Such woods are sanded at a slight angle to the grain to avoid enlarging the individual pores of the wood. The grains of abrasive, which pass through the

Top: The easiest way to sand the end-grain of wood is to clamp the board between two pieces of scrap wood, with the edges all flush. *Left:* Flutes can be sanded by folding the sandpaper and using as if it were a file. *Right:* The "shoe-shine" technique for sanding will work well on difficult turnings.

elongated pores running parallel to the length, tend to round or flare the edges, making them larger and more difficult to fill. This leaves the surface rough, and in some cases even changes the pattern of the grain.

The handiest size piece of abrasive paper for normal sanding is the quarter sheet. You can easily cut all but the coarsest abrasive sheets to size with an old pair of scissors. Otherwise, sandpaper can be torn into desired sizes by folding the sheet into quarters, creasing the folds, then tearing the paper carefully along the creased folds.

The abrasive used when rough sanding may leave fine scratches over the entire surface of the wood. The smaller abrasive particles of medium-grit papers will remove these scratches, in turn leaving a pattern of finer marks,

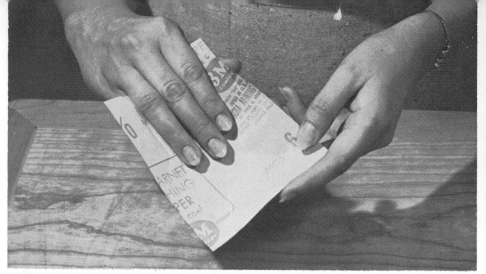

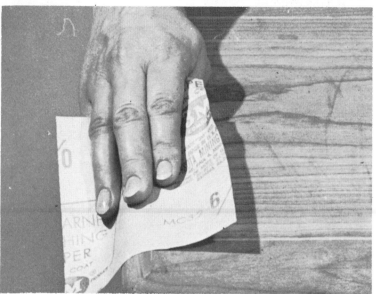

When sanding shaped surface sandpaper must be held by the thumb and last finger on the abrasive, while other fingers hold together on other side. If sanding is done without a block of wood, around which a paper usually wraps, unusual care should be taken to keep sanding power constant, thus preventing low spots or unevenness.

or scratches. One works with the grain as in rough sanding, with the exception previously discussed. Continue this operation until all first-operation scratch marks have been removed. A fine-grit paper is then used for the finishing.

The use of fine-grit papers can bring the wood to a degree of smoothness which is capable of reflecting oblique light. To examine the work surface, hold its horizontally toward a light source at a point a few inches below eye level. Many experienced refinishers lightly pass the tips of their fingers over the surface in order to be able to detect slight ridges or other imperfections, but any minor ridges or other irregularities will also show up quite clearly in oblique light, and they can be outlined with penciled guide lines. After these irregularities are removed, the process is repeated until the reflection of light is uniform over the whole surface.

Before this final sanding with very fine finishing paper, many finishers dampen the wood with a sponge to raise the grain. After drying, a thin wash of shellac, sanding sealer, or sizing is applied to stiffen the raised fibers (or *whiskers*, as these are sometimes called). The raised grain is then sanded smooth and sometimes the procedure is repeated. This extra step will prevent the grain from being raised by bleach, water, stain, and the like.

When working with open-grained woods which require staining and

Above: Before the final sanding, cracks should be filled with a stick shellac matching final color of the piece. *Below:* Knots should be sealed with coat of clear white shellac.

filling, some finishers prefer to apply stain and filler, let them dry, and then do the final sanding. In some instances, this procedure may be used instead of the process of sponging the surface to bring up the grain and applying the wash coat of shellac or sanding sealer. When sanding the stained and filled wood, it is necessary to apply a few drops of rubbing oil to the sanding pad frequently in order to prevent clogging of the paper. Moreover, a very light stroke must be used to avoid cutting through the stain and exposing bare wood.

The wood dust produced by sanding with a close-coat paper will become packed between the abrasive particles and reduce their cutting action. This is not a problem with open-coat papers because the particles are so widely

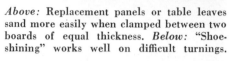

Above: Replacement panels or table leaves sand more easily when clamped between two boards of equal thickness. *Below:* "Shoe-shining" works well on difficult turnings.

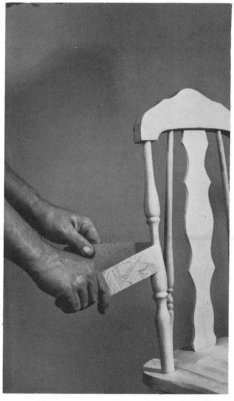

Some refinishers deliberately raise grain before final sanding (*above*) or use steel wool instead of sandpaper between finishes.

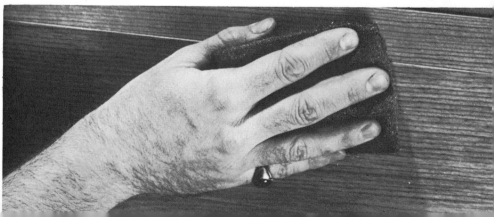

distributed that the abrasive is virtually self-cleaning. However, the use of open-coated papers may produce rather pronounced scratch patterns, and it is therefore advisable to use a close-coat paper for all steps which follow rough sanding.

Some finishers tack or clamp a scrub brush to the end of their workbench, and clean the paper by running the sanding block over the bristles to renew cutting action; others prefer to use a finer brush, since it is less likely to damage the abrasive surface. Wood dust will also clog the pores in the wood. This dust may tend to dull or cloud the finish if it is not removed. The best way to clean sanded wood is by using the dusting attachment of a vacuum cleaner; run over the surface frequently with the brush attachment to prevent the dust from working down into the pores.

BLEACHING

Once the old finish has been removed and the surface has been smoothed by sanding, the wood may need to be lightened. On some woods this can be done by applying a semi-transparent toner or a pigmented stain; on others, the color of the wood itself can be changed, within limits, by bleaching. Toners and pigmented stains tend to reduce the grain in varying degrees. For this reason, finishers often choose to bleach the wood; however, skilled craftsmen usually cautiously approach the decision to use a bleach. A fair rule of thumb is, if the piece is made from one of the finer cabinet woods and it is highly valued, bleach should not be used; the results could be quite disappointing.

Many bleaches involve two operations—applying and then neutralizing—but some are single-application types, for which two solutions are mixed (*above*), applied together.

When the entire surface of the wood is lightened without attempting to change the natural color variation, bleach may be considered as a counterpart to penetrating stain. Like the stain, it changes the color of the very thin layer of wood at the surface. Some of the finer cabinet woods (such as walnut, cherry, and the mahoganies) do not bleach well under the ordinary procedures, particularly when bleach is used on old pieces made from these woods.

If the finisher discovers, after the old finish is removed, that two or more different kinds of wood were used in the construction, he can probably match them quite closely if he bleaches the darker wood. Discolorations and stains which are the result of normal wear can generally be removed by bleaching, although on an antique some of these, at least, can be retained as usage marks. Sometimes the grain contrast may be too strong and, in some cases, this contrast can be toned down with bleach.

Mineral streaks and certain sap streaks which do not respond to bleach can be covered with a light pigmented stain to match the rest of the wood. Highly resinous woods rarely bleach satisfactorily. To lighten these woods, a toner or pigmented stain should be used.

A saturated solution of oxalic acid in hot water is strong enough for bleaching the ordinary, lighter-colored woods and for removing discolorations. This solution can be neutralized by using plain white vinegar, or a solution made by dissolving one ounce of borax in one quart of water. For tougher jobs, one of the two-solution commercial peroxide-type bleaches can

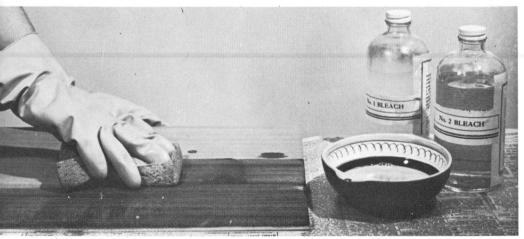

Above: Apply bleach with grain. *Below left:* Then rinse surface to remove residue. Cover unbleachable streaks with pigmented stain or opaque finish matching wood (*below right*).

be used if the manufacturer's instructions for neutralizing are followed.

The finisher should wear rubber gloves, old clothes, and keep his eyes protected from spatters when using any bleach. If the bleach solution drops on the skin, it should be washed off immediately. The instructions on the container pertaining to handling and application must be followed closely. Bleach can be applied with a cellulose sponge, a fiber-bristle brush, or rubber sponge. A bleach must never—but never—be applied to shellacked, lacquered, or varnished surfaces because spontaneous combustion can occur. Bleaches should be used only on bare wood. Common household bleaches (Clorox, for example, or Purex) can also be used with fair success on some woods, though they generally must be mixed in much stronger proportions than if they were to be used for the purposes for which they are normally intended. It is necessary to experiment to find the right concentration for each job. After these bleaches have dried, a borax solution should be used as a neutralizer.

Two-solution bleaches can be used either consecutively or premixed, according to the manufacturer's instructions. Some require complete drying of the first solution before the second is applied; others stipulate a certain length of time between applications. The wood to be bleached should be clean and dry, and the bleach must be applied evenly, following the direction of the grain. For easy-to-bleach woods, a single application of both solutions, either together or separately, may be sufficient. When a light color is desired, further application of the second solution may be necessary. However, enough time must be allowed for the initial application to take effect before more is applied.

Some bleaches require a neutralizer (usually plain vinegar); others do not. Even if neutralizing is not specified, it is best to sponge the surface lightly with water after the bleaching operation is complete to remove any residue. Allow at least 24 hours for drying before proceeding with the finishing; insufficient drying may cause pinholing and lack of adhesion in the finishing materials.

Once the desired color has been achieved by bleaching, care must be taken not to spoil it by incorrect application of a filler. While the filler will impart some color (mainly to the pores of the wood) with only a slight staining action over the rest of the surface, it can darken the entire surface if it isn't wiped carefully.

Some bleached surfaces will darken with age, especially when they are exposed to direct sunlight for long periods of time. (The ultraviolet rays of the sun tend to cause a reversal of the bleaching action.) To avoid this, bleached pieces must be kept out of direct sunlight as much as possible. Lacquers which have a high percentage of synthetic resins reduce this effect, since these resins filter out ultraviolet rays. Even with this protective finish, however, it is best to avoid exposure to direct sunlight.

IV

Staining, Filling, and Sealing

Though it is never mentioned in finishing schedules, patience is one of the most important ingredients in any new finish. Often an hour or two of extra drying time, an extra half-hour of sanding, and full follow-through on every step can mean the difference between a top-rate professional finish and a near disaster.

When a professional finisher is at work he often gives the impression that he is unduly fussy about detail, and that he isn't getting anywhere. Actually, he is just applying a finish on schedule and taking his time, knowing full well what the final result will be; in other words, he knows precisely what he is doing.

There are two main reasons for finishing wood—for protection and beauty. Today's trend is toward transparent finishes which bring out the natural beauty of grain and figure. But what about those plain, secondary woods which do not match the natural beauty of the finer cabinet woods but have equal or even greater structural strength? Stripping the finish from an old chest may reveal several kinds of wood underneath, because the use of several woods was common practice among builders of plain, utilitarian pieces which were to be painted or stained a dark color. Usually it is preferable to use an opaque, or painted, finish to renew such a piece, although some pieces can be refinished satisfactorily by using a stain finish in the darker shades.

The three operations covered in this chapter prepare the wood for the final finishing coats. Proper staining brings the wood to the desired color; filling emphasizes grain and provides a smooth, even foundation on which to build the top coats; sealing protects the wood, filler, and stain, and provides a surface to which the top coats will bond.

The first three steps in applying a typical transparent finish to an open-grain wood exploit the beauty of the grain and at the same time provide a foundation for the protective finish that follows, which usually consists of base and top coats. On some close-grain woods, the filler and sealer can be omitted, especially when using certain newer synthetics. When an opaque finish is used on close-grained woods, a stain and sealer generally are not used.

STAINING

If a transparent finish is to be used, and if the color of the wood is to be changed or the grain contrast built up, staining is usually the first step in the finishing operation. A stain consists of a coloring medium (either aniline dye or a pigment) which is dissolved or suspended in a solvent. Ready-mixed stains may be purchased, or the color may be obtained separately in powder form and then mixed. While all stains penetrate the surface of the wood to a greater or lesser degree, penetrating stains go much deeper than pigment or wiping stains. They change the color of the wood itself by changing its light-reflecting properties. The depth of penetration is increased if the stain is slightly warm when it is applied. Many pigment stains contain a small amount of penetrating stain in order to assure even color.

Stain in itself can not always make one wood look like another. Some pieces of cherry can be stained walnut color, and the result can be remarkably realistic. Certain other woods, such as black willow, lend themselves to such deception well. But pine colored with a walnut stain does not look like walnut, because it does not have the grain or texture to take a walnut-colored stain. It must be understood that each wood has a color of its own, that different woods have different rates of absorption, and that the differences between springwood and summerwood are more pronounced in some varieties than in others.

Same stain reacts in different ways to different woods. To be sure that the end product will be what is desired, always test stain on concealed parts of piece being refinished.

Any color of stain may be used on any wood, regardless of the wood mentioned in the name of the stain; for example, a "walnut" stain can be used on other woods. However, when stain is being used to match the colors of two different kinds of woods, you may have to alter it in some cases by diluting, mixing with other stains, or by adding very small amounts of powder stain to it. Although it is possible to match color in this way, the character of the wood still will not be changed and the results may be disappointing. To be sure of successful results, a check should be made on a test panel.

Stains should be thought of as color tints. Although a little practice is required, it is possible to custom-mix stains to give just the right shade for each particular job. Stains made by dissolving aniline powder in solvent (the true "wood dyes") are commonly classified according to the solvent used in their preparation—water, oil, spirit (alcohol) and lacquer reducer, or thinner. Two additional types should be included in this group since they also use aniline colors dissolved in solvent and are transparent colors: non-grain-raising (NGR) stains, which closely resemble water stains, employing a glycol solvent in place of water; and shading stains, which are spirit or lacquer stains containing varying amounts of color pigment, with a binder added to give them body. Shading stain is used between finishing coats to give shaded effects or to conceal undesirable grain contrast, streaks in the wood and, sometimes, to achieve a hand-rubbed effect on panels.

Pigmented stains or wiping stains are really very thin paints made by mixing colors ground in oil with turpentine, linseed oil, naphtha, or other reducers. Such stains tend to obscure the grain, and are quite widely used for reducing the contrast between springwood and summerwood, or between different woods. They are also used for shading and antiquing. They should be thinned with naphtha or the thinner specified in the manufacturer's instructions for use on hardwoods.

A third group, water-soluble vegetable stains, was once very popular but has now largely been replaced by water-aniline stains. *Water stains* are economical, non-fading, and offer brilliant colors which penetrate deeply but evenly. They will not bleed into the finishing coats. Their one major drawback is that the water in which the color is dissolved will sometimes loosen glued joints, or they cause the grain of the wood to raise, making it necessary to give the surface a very light sanding after the stain has been applied.

Water stains can be applied with either a spray gun or brush. When brushing, the work must be done skillfully to avoid lap marks; spraying usually yields better results. Water stains usually dry to recoat in twelve hours, but can be force-dried with heat in four to six hours. Water stains are available in powdered form only, because water is usually easy to obtain and the mixing process is quite simple. This should be tried on test panels first, and the gun adjusted to give just the coverage and uniformity wanted. The stain will penetrate better if it is slightly warm when applied. This holds true for both brushing and spraying.

Since water stain will raise the grain of the wood, it is necessary to dampen the surface and sand carefully before staining. This step will not entirely eliminate the problem of raised grain, but it will reduce the amount of sanding required after the water stain dries, with less chance of cutting through that thin layer of stained wood when removing whiskers.

End grain presents a problem with any type of stain. It is much "thirstier" than surface grain, and may turn out several shades darker than the rest of the piece. To prevent this, apply a very thin wash of white (clear) shellac taking special care not to get any of the wash on the flat grain. Another successful method is to sponge water onto the end grain immediately before applying the stain.

The two former methods also work well when a great variation is likely in the absorption rate on different areas of the same surface, as on sapwood, springwood, and summerwood.

When grooved surfaces or ornamental carvings are being stained, somewhat less stain is applied than to flat surfaces. After the stain dries and the result is noted, a second or even a third application can be made, if necessary, to get the right color. Some finishers apply a thin wash of shellac to such surfaces before staining.

One trick used in water staining with a brush is that of following the brush closely with a soft cloth. In this way several applications may have to be made, but color depth can be controlled with a greater degree of certainty. A soft varnish brush should be used with water stains. In this case, an old brush is better than a new one because the ferrule and bristle butts will be well sealed with varnish and are less likely to be damaged by prolonged use in water. The brush should be cleaned with turpentine and then washed well with soap and water before it is used in stain.

If at all possible, stains, especially water stains, should be applied on a horizontal surface. The stain must be brushed on with the grain of the wood, with long, sweeping strokes. It is best to work back and forth over the surface without lifting the brush. In the application of any stain, the work must be done quickly and the brush must be kept well-filled. After the surface has been covered evenly with stain, shake out the brush and brush out the stain coat with long smooth strokes, following the grain. Allow at least twelve hours for drying (note manufacturer's instructions), and then sand the surface lightly. On water-stained surfaces a very thin wash of shellac will stiffen the raised fibers so that they will sand off more readily.

The resins in some soft woods make it difficult to achieve a uniform stain. In such cases, sponge the surface with alcohol to remove surface resins and add a little vinegar to the stain to increase penetration. Warming the stain slightly before applications will increase its penetrating power.

Non-grain-raising (NGR) stains have all the good points and none of the disadvantages of water stains. The fast-drying glycol solvent which is used in place of water will not raise the grain; however, the fast-drying characteristics of this type stain make it somewhat more difficult to apply with a brush. If a brush is used, it is necessary to buy a brushing-or-spraying grade stain. The drying action of most NGR stains can also be slowed down a bit with the addition of about ten per cent Carbitor or Cellusolve, but even so, the stain surface dries quite rapidly.

The best way to obtain a uniform color when brushing is to use a large brush and to apply a very wet coat. The cutting-in technique may be fine for varnish, but with NGR stain the edges will be dry before the surface is covered. It is best when staining a small table to start in one corner and carry the stain from side to side, all the way out to the edges; then wipe it immediately with a soft cloth to even out the color and remove any excess. The trick is to get the stain on fast so that you are always working toward a wet edge; then it should be wiped immediately. Larger surfaces can often be broken into smaller areas suitable for working in this manner. On some woods, NGR stains will raise the grain very slightly but, nevertheless, will give an even color.

If there is danger of not producing a lap-free job, play it safe and dilute the stain to half-strength by adding an equal amount of solvent. By applying two coats of this weak stain, and following closely with a cloth, you will achieve the same result with no trouble at the lap. Another way is to wash the work quickly with the stain solvent and immediately apply a single coat of full-strength stain. This is not necessarily a recommended procedure, but, if done quickly, it can produce a reasonably good job. NGR stain should be sprayed in a moderately light coat, not too wet. A small spray pattern should be used, but it should be fanned out by holding the gun somewhat farther from the surface than when spraying opaques. By spraying a heavier coat on light parts of the wood and a lighter coat on dark portions, the finisher can control the over-all color and maintain uniformity. Always have a good light near the work surface so that you can properly evaluate the color depth.

Most NGR stains dry to recoat in three hours or less. Since they are available in a variety of ready-mixed colors, little or nothing is to be gained from buying the stain and solvent separately for home mixing.

Spirit stains are among the most rapid-drying of any stains, drying to recoat in 15 to 30 minutes. Used extensively for patching and touch-up work, they are made by dissolving aniline dyes in alcohol. They can be purchased in powder form or ready-mixed with various blended solvents. Because they dry so quickly, spirit stains should be applied with a spray gun, although they may tend to raise the grain slightly even when sprayed, if applied when the humidity is above normal.

It is possible to apply spirit stain by brush without leaving brush marks. The addition of a small amount of shellac gives a little more body to the stain and slows drying time somewhat. To brush on a spirit stain, the finisher must work fast—very fast—to get it on without laps. A spirit-stained surface is subject to fading and should not be exposed to strong sunlight until it has been protected with a coat of sealer.

Shading stains are first cousins to spirit stains. These stains are made by dissolving stain powder in alcohol or lacquer thinner, then adding a little shellac for body. They are usually sprayed between top coats to achieve a shaded, or rubbed, effect. They are sometimes used to mask sap streaks or certain other imperfections. Like ordinary spirit stains, they are very fast-drying—some can be recoated in 60 seconds or less—and are available in either ready-mixed or powder forms.

Penetrating oil stains are made by dissolving aniline colors in a light oil (turpentine, naphtha, benzol, or gasoline) and can be purchased in powder or ready-mixed form. They penetrate well but rather unevenly in some woods, going deeper into soft spots in the surface. Penetrating oil stains are not quite as fade-resistant as water stains, but are more fade-resistant than spirit stains.

The main advantage of the *oil stain* is its ease of application. It makes little difference whether you use a brush or spray gun because the color is controlled by the length of time the stain is left on the surface before wiping rather than by the thickness of the coat. Quick wiping produces a lighter color; the longer the stain remains on the surface the greater is the depth of the color.

The stain is wiped while still wet, but only after it has remained on the surface long enough for penetration to begin. If the surface is wiped across the grain when the stain is too dry, streaking will sometimes occur; therefore, it should always be wiped with the grain. Oil stains will bleed because of the solvents used, but the worst of this can be avoided if the oil-stained surface is sealed with a wash coat of shellac. This is one of the simplest stains to apply. The important rule to remember is that the same amount of time must be allowed before wiping on all sections of the same job.

With the exception of shading stains, the foregoing five stains are wood dyes, because the colors in them dissolve completely in the solvent and are absorbed by the wood.

Pigment oil stains contain tiny particles of color pigment rather than dissolved colors. Like penetrating oil stain, it is slow-drying and easy to apply. The pigment coloring settles to the bottom of the can, and the stain must be stirred well before applying. A cloth or brush is used to apply pigmented stain. After the stain has been applied to the surface of the wood, it should be allowed to dry for five to ten minutes. It should then be wiped with a soft cloth to remove all of the stain which will come off when wiped under moderate pressure. Shade, or depth of the color, depends on the length of time the stain is left on and on how much pressure is used when wiping. When using pigment oil stain on softwoods (for example, fir, pine, and poplar), a thin wash coat of shellac is often applied prior to the stain to make wiping easier.

Blonding, or lightening the color of the wood without bleaching, is possible with pigmented stain because this stain is actually a thin paint. Clean wiping should be the rule; this automatically limits the color range to moderate lightening of the original wood color. It is foolish to attempt to make a blond out of such a wood as black walnut. However, on naturally light woods, such as maple and birch, a blond finish is easily obtained with white or tinted wiping stains.

Interesting color effects can be obtained by tinting white-pigment wiping stain with a little oil color. This can be mixed separately with turpentine and then added to the stain, a little at a time, until the desired color is obtained. With this, and with all other stains as well, it is preferable to use a test panel because the color of the wiped stain is usually several shades lighter than the stain itself.

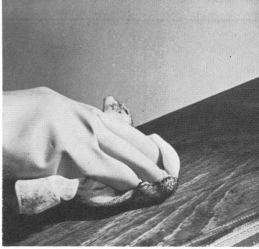

Apply wiping stain with lint-free cloth until surface looks dry, stain is evenly blended.

In its broadest definition, *toning* means covering the surface of the wood with a light-colored semi-transparent undercoat; in this sense, blonding with a light pigmented stain can be considered toning. However, most toners are lacquer-based and are more transparent than pigmented stains. A good toner can be made by adding one part white lacquer to four or five parts clear flat lacquer. When sprayed directly on the bare wood, this mixture makes the wood much lighter without obscuring the grain.

The following are a few helpful hints on staining which will make the job easier and faster:

—Apply a very thin wash coat of shellac to porous woods before staining. This will make them less "thirsty," and will assure a more uniform color.

—Test the stain on a hidden part of the work, or on a test panel of the same kind of wood.

—Plan the job in steps, staining one area at a time.

—Treat knots and sapwood with one or more coats of alcohol to increase their rate of absorption.

—Dilute the stain with the proper solvent or reducer, if you wish to lighten the color.

—Be especially careful with end grain so that it doesn't turn out darker than the surface. Control absorption with shellac wash by using a drier brush, or by diluting the stain with solvent.

Many finishers apply a wash coat of shellac before filling open-grain woods. This seals the stain and gives a sharp edge to the pores, making wiping easier. However, some finishers use a colored, or tinted, filler and follow this with a prepared sealer. The sealer can be omitted on natural-finish woods.

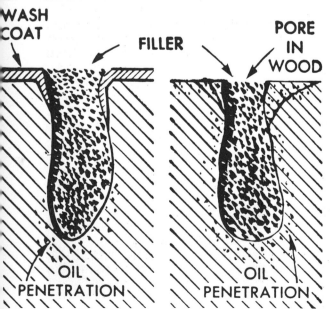

Applying thin wash coat of shellac to open-grain woods before filling sharpens and seals edges of pores, makes the job much more efficient.

If the work is wash-coated, the filler is confined exclusively to the pores of the wood. If it is not wash-coated, the oil or coloring pigment in the filler will penetrate the surface of the wood and act as a stain which, if not wiped carefully, can produce an undesirable monotone finish which lacks contrast and luster. The wash coat must never be so heavy that it partially fills the pores. When properly applied, a wash coat over stain is invisible.

FILLING

Wood having large pores requires application of a paste wood filler to build a level surface on which top finishing coats are to be applied. Although the liquid fillers may be used for denser woods, they are not always suitable; diluted paste fillers are safer. In addition to leveling the surface of open-grained woods, the filler plays an important role by either emphasizing or de-emphasizing the grain. To retain the grain contrast

Liquid filler is essentially only a varnish with a small amount of silex added. Liquid filler can be applied to close-grained wood only. First apply with a short-bristle brush with the grain (*above*). Then, to be sure of penetration, end by cross-brushing (*right*).

of the unfinished wood, the color of the filler should be a shade or two darker than the stained color of the wood. Sometimes a very dark filler is used to provide even more contrast. White and brightly-colored fillers, which are used for novelty effects, also emphasize the grain.

Paste filler is made by mixing silex (powdered rock quartz) with raw linseed oil and a drying agent. This basic untinted mixture is known commercially as "natural" filler. Earth pigments ground into oil are added to achieve the stock shades of ready-mixed fillers. Paste filler must be thinned to brushing consistency with either naphtha, which shortens the drying time, or turpentine, which lengthens it, or with a mixture of the two. The addition of a small amount of boiled linseed oil will hold the coat open for thirty minutes or more; adding a little japan drier will make it set more quickly.

Paste fillers should be applied with a short-bristle brush at a slight angle to grain of wood (*above*), then towed-off with burlap to assure penetration and remove excess (*below*).

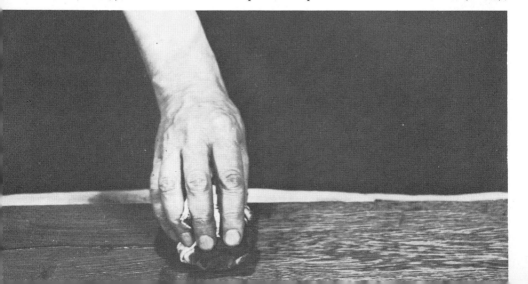

It is necessary to mix and thin paste fillers properly. *Right:* Empty the filler paste into a clean container about twice as large as filler's can. *Above:* Mix thoroughly with naphtha. See proportions given in table below.

The consistency of the filler will depend on the size of the pores to be filled. In general, the larger the pores are, the thicker the mixture should be within the limits of brush application. The relative terms used to describe the different consistencies of fillers are unnecessarily confusing: the heavy mix is not actually a heavy-bodied material; its consistency is about the same (or a little heavier) than that of varnish. The following table lists the filler mixes commonly used for popular furniture woods:

Filler Mix for Various Woods

No Filler Needed	Thin Filler	Medium Filler	Heavy Filler
Basswood	Alder	Butternut	Ash
Cedar	Beech	Mahogany	Chestnut
Fir	Birch	Orientalwood	Kelobra
Pine	Boxwood	Prima Vera	Locust
Poplar	Cherry	Purpleheart	Mahogany (Phil.)
Spruce	Gum	Rosewood	Oak
Willow	Maple	Walnut	Teak

The first step in mixing filler is breaking up the heavy material in the can with a putty knife. Then add a very small amount of thinner, and stir until thoroughly mixed. After this initial mixing, larger amounts of thinner should be added and stirred in until the mix reaches the proper consistency.

Mix only enough filler for the job at hand because the thinned filler will thicken again in a few hours. Various quantities of filler can be mixed, as outlined in the following chart:

Proportions for Mixing Various Quantities of Filler

Heavy Mix (16-lb. Base)

Approx. Amt. Needed *	Paste	Thinner
2 Gals.	16 lbs.	1 Gal.
5 Pts.	5 lbs.	2½ Pts.
2 Qts.	1 Qt.	1 Qt.
2 Pts.	1 Pt.	1 Pt.
1 Pt.	1 lb.	½ Pt.
½ Pt.	½ lb.	4 oz.

Medium Mix (12-lb. Base)

Approx. Amt. Needed *	Paste	Thinner
1 Gal., 3 Qts.	12 lbs.	1 Gal.
3 Qts.	5 lbs.	3 Pts., 5 oz.
2 Qts., 10 oz.	1 Qt.	2 Pts., 10 oz.
1 Qt., 5 oz.	1 Pt.	1 Pt., 5 oz.
1 Pt., 2 oz.	1 lb.	10½ oz.
9 oz.	½ lb.	5¼ oz.

Thin Mix (8-lb. Base)

Approx. Amt. Needed *	Paste	Thinner
1½ Gals.	8 lbs.	1 Gal.
1 Gal.	5 lbs.	5 Pts.
3 Qts.	1 Qt.	2 Qts.
3 Pts.	1 Pt.	2 Pts.
1½ Pts.	1 lb.	1 Pt.
12 oz.	½ lb.	½ Pt.

* One pint thinned filler covers approx. 35 sq. ft.

Use naphtha for thinning when you want the filler to set up more quickly. Turpentine will hold the coat open longer. If you wish to experiment, the two liquids may be mixed together until exactly the right proportions to obtain the desired result are found. To hold the coat open for thirty or forty minutes, a small amount of boiled linseed oil can be added. To make a very quick-setting filler, add a small amount of japan drier.

Commercial *liquid fillers* are simply varnishes with a small amount of silex added; they are designed for use with close-grained woods. The consistency of these products depends on the type of varnish used and the amount of silex added.

A short-bristle brush is the best applicator for fillers. The filler should be applied liberally, and brushed thoroughly at a slight angle with the grain. Even with a slow-drying filler, not more than eight to ten square feet should be covered; otherwise, the wiping and cleaning-up operations will get out of hand. As soon as dull spots appear on the surface, the filler is ready for wiping. Do not wait until the whole surface becomes dull; this usually indicates that the filler is too dry for easy removal of the excess.

Padding-in, which is the first step in removing surplus filler, is intended to force the filler into the pores. Using a felt block or smooth cloth pad, the surface is wiped with a circular motion primarily across the grain. The pad should not be lifted because this is likely to pull filler from the pores. Many finishers omit this step altogether on some woods, and proceed directly to towing-off. *Towing-off* is the process which packs the filler into the pores and removes the excess in one operation. Burlap or any other coarse fabric may be used. The wiping motion is always across the grain; the pad should be turned and refolded continuously. The finisher cleans the surface thoroughly, moving from one end of the work to the other. If the filler has set up and is too hard for easy wiping, the pad should be moistened with naphtha. In extreme cases, another coat of filler should be brushed on; this will soften the first coat and permit easier wiping.

Wiping lightly at a slight angle with the grain of the wood removes any slight traces of filler which still remain after towing-off. Any soft, lintless cloth can be used for the final wiping operation. The cloth can be moistened slightly with benzine if necessary. Inside corners and other spots which are hard to reach can be wiped clean with a picking stick. A scrubbing brush can be used to remove excess filler from intricate carvings. In any case, however, neither of these methods is used unless normal wiping is impossible.

Drying time varies from six hours for quick-drying fillers to 36 hours for slow-drying fillers. When the filler is dry, it should be sealed with a light coat of shellac or a prepared sanding sealer. After the sealer dries, sand it lightly to remove any ridges. Then give the work a full-bodied coat of varnish for varnish finishes, or lacquer sealer for lacquer finishes. This second coat of sealer will fill any tiny open pores. It should be sanded thoroughly to a flat, smooth surface. Top coats of varnish or lacquer are then applied to complete the finish.

Several common filler defects can be easily remedied. *Pinholes* are usually caused by the use of filler which is so thick that it bridges the pores. The trapped gas in the pores then explodes forming a miniature crater. This can be avoided by using a thinner filler. Do not use japan in mixing and dust the work thoroughly before filling.

If a filler is not given enough time to dry, or if a filler was used under lacquer which was not suitable for such use, a defect called *raised grain* will result. The former is solved by allowing the filler ample drying time. Then, before and after staining, sand off the surface fuzz with 5/0 paper.

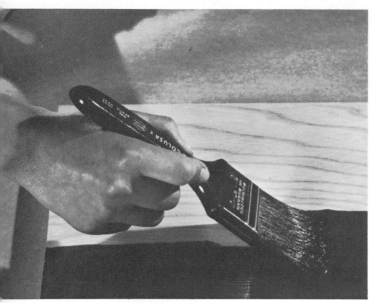

Staining filler may be applied with either a short-bristle brush (*left*) or by wiping with a clean, lint-free cloth. When using cloth (*above; below left*) apply filler with circular motion with the grain.

After applying filler wait until dry spots appear on surface (*above right*)—as refinishers would say, when it "flats off." If ready, filler rolls up into a ball when finger is drawn over wood (*below left*). Then pad in with burlap, in circular motion (*below right*).

Gray pores occur if excess moisture is present in the wood, if the filler has not dried sufficiently, or if the filler applied was too light in color. Checking the moisture content of the wood, and always using a filler as dark or darker than the stain remedies this defect.

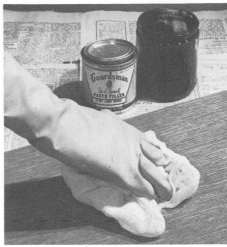

After the excess filler has been wiped from the surface with a coarse cloth (*above left*), final wiping should be given with the grain, using soft, lint-free cloth (*above right*).

If a filler is not cleaned off completely, this can cause a *streaked* or *cloudy finish*. This also can be the result of using wood turpentine instead of gum turpentine when mixing the filler. To avoid this flaw, use gum turpentine or naphtha when mixing the filler, and moisten the wiping rag with naphtha for the final wiping of the filler coat.

A few precautions to keep in mind when working with filler are as follows:

—The filler should not be too heavy. It should be fluid enough to sink to the bottom of the pores.

—The same brand of filler should be mixed the same way every time— for each part of the job.

—Sufficient drying time must be allowed. Most fillers are commonly described as either "four-hour," or "overnight dry," but it is advisable to increase such minimum times by about half again as much time. The extremely fast-drying fillers which are now available are ready for the top coat in fifteen or twenty minutes but, even with these, it is best to allow an extra ten or fifteen minutes.

—It is safest to use the standard manufactured paste fillers made of silex and oil. Unless a finisher owns or operates a furniture factory, there is no point in mixing his own filler. Homemade mixes involving vegetable matter, such as corn starch, should never be used because these mixtures are often far from inert under the top coats which follow.

In one sense, all woods require filling. Even nonporous, close-grained woods have minute grooves and depressions in their surfaces, although these are too small to be filled with a regular silex-base filler. A sealer coat, when applied directly over bare wood or stain to protect the surface, also fills these depressions and thus serves as a filler.

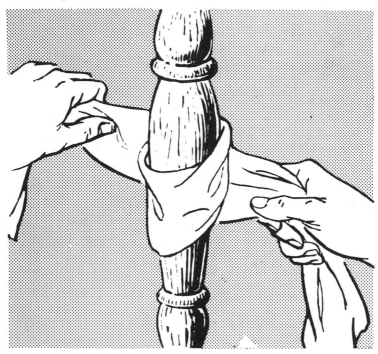

"Tow off" turning by wrapping cloth around it, pulling quickly back and forth.

SEALING

If the solvent of the finishing coat is the same as that used in the filler or stain, and the top coats are applied directly over these materials, the filler will be softened and the stain will be dissolved, bleeding into the finishing coat and leaving a muddy appearance. Thus, a sealer is used as an undercoat to protect these materials or, if no stain is used, to protect the wood from discoloration. Because this same problem can arise between stain and filler applications, the stain is also sealed. In addition to protecting the stain, this sealer hardens to a sharp edge on the rim of the pores and makes wiping easier. The most popular sealer is a wash coat of shellac, white for a natural or light-colored finish, and orange for a darker finish. Shellac when combined with a mixing lacquer is slightly more durable; it is growing in popularity as a sealer because it dries faster (in approximately two hours). Sealers must be sanded before the top coats are applied.

Lacquer sealers dry very rapidly (in about twenty minutes). They are made by adding a sanding medium to clear lacquer, and were developed for use with lacquer finishes. They can be brushed, but are more easily applied with a spray gun.

Special *resin sealers* are designed for use on softwoods. Because of the great difference in texture between the hard summer growth and softer spring growth, the first coat of stain applied will penetrate unevenly; this greatly over-emphasizes the grain. When the resin sealer is applied before staining, it makes the penetration more even, which results in a more subdued grain. As previously mentioned, it also acts as a filler for softwoods, filling in the minute depressions and grooves which occur even in woods which are non-porous.

Penetrating wood sealers are short-cut synthetic finishing materials which combine sealing, finishing, and sometimes even staining, into one operation. Normally applied to new wood, they can also be used in refinishing if all the old finish has been completely removed. Surfaces must be thoroughly sanded before the penetrating sealers are applied. After the surface is dusted, the sealer is applied with a cloth. Usually, the first coat soaks into the wood immediately, so additional coats should be applied until the wood can not absorb any more. After 24 hours have been allowed for drying time, two to four additional coats are applied to build a finish, each of which is rubbed with steel wool. The last coat may be rubbed with pumice and oil to obtain a satin sheen.

This type of sealer may also be used on open-grain woods. Follow the same procedure, but apply a paste filler after the first coat. The sealer should be dry to the touch before the filler is applied; however, if the sealer is completely dry, it will be difficult to force the filler into the pores.

Plywood sealers were developed to overcome some of the special difficulties which arise when finishing fir plywood. Ordinary finishes do not work well on fir plywood because it has a pronounced grain and because the wood tends to fuzz and face-check. Phenolic resin primer, commonly known as plywood sealer, is usually marketed under a trade name, such as Firzite or Rex, and is used for sealing pine and fir, as well as plywood. These sealers are also supplied in pigmented white for use on plywood.

A brush, spray gun, or cloth pad may be used to apply plywood sealer. The bare wood should be given a full, wet coat. After it has dried for a few minutes, the surface should be wiped clean with a soft cloth. The sealer will be dry enough for handling almost immediately, but should dry over-night before any finishing material is applied.

If a dark-stained finish is desired, use a pigmented oil stain over the sealer. The clear sealer can also be mixed with colors-in-oil to darken the surface. Although the clear sealer may be mixed with white paint for limed effects on fir plywood, it is better to use prepared sealer for this purpose.

V

The Finishing Touch

A good finish not only protects the wood, but, properly applied, intensifies the grain and the natural color, even though the color depth has been changed by staining. As in sanding, staining, and filling, the best insurance against failure when applying finishes is painstaking care and resisting the tendency to rush through one or more steps because they seem unimportant. A beautiful finish is simply the result of a determination to follow through every detail of the schedule.

All the preceding materials—stains, fillers, and sealers—are used to color the wood and prepare it for a protective finish. In furniture finishing, the most popular protective materials are the three transparent finishes: varnish (which includes shellac), lacquer, and synthetic finishes.

OIL VARNISHES

All *varnishes* contain resins which dry to produce a hard, lustrous finish. While there are three main types of varnish, only two of them are used by themselves as finishes. The third, japan varnish, resembles oil varnish, but contains more japan, which is a drying agent. Although never used for a finishing coat, japan is added to oil varnishes to shorten the drying time.

Oil varnish has four main ingredients: a blend of resins to give a hard finish; a vehicle, or drying oil (either linseed oil or Chinawood oil), which hardens by oxidation and acts as a binder for the resins making the varnish film more elastic; a volatile solvent (generally turpentine) used to thin the varnish for easier application; and a drier which shortens the drying time because the drying oil oxidizes very slowly. Those varnishes which contain a large percentage of drying oils are commonly known as "long-oil" varnishes, while those containing a smaller percentage of such oils are called "short-oil" varnishes.

Generally, the greater the percentage of drying oils in a finish, the more elastic and durable it is, but the drying time required is longer accordingly. Quicker-drying, short-oil varnishes give a harder, more brittle finish. Unlike long-oil varnishes, these varnishes can be sanded without gumming. Rubbing-and-polishing varnishes and polishing varnishes are short-oil varnishes which contain very hard resins. They are manufactured especially for top coats used in fine furniture finishing. Spar varnish, table-top varnish, and bar-top varnishes are slow-drying, long-oil varnishes which give a tough, elastic finish with more resistance to water, heat, scratching, and general wear.

Most clear finishing materials are ready for use directly from the can, but some of them may be a trifle heavy. A rough estimate of the amount you will need should be poured into a separate container and thinned a little at a time until it has reached the correct brushing consistency. After the job is done, any of the varnish left in this container should be discarded. This procedure will eliminate any chance contamination of the contents of the can with dust, brush bristles, or similar material.

Like oil, varnish flows best when at a warm temperature—between seventy and eighty degrees; at this temperature, it should level about ten to twenty minutes after application. The flow should be checked before the job is begun. Poor flow, which is caused by low temperature, can be corrected by placing the varnish in a pan of hot (100°) water for a few minutes. Never place it over an open flame.

Dust is the enemy of any finish until it has dried. Varnish, therefore, should be applied in a place which is as dust-free as possible. No matter how much care is taken, however, dust specks will get on the finish. These can be lifted from the wet varnish with a clean sliver of wood to which the specks will cling when touched lightly. Don't wait until the varnish is tacky; specks should always be removed as soon as they are noticed. Another way of lifting dust specks is to use burnt varnish, which consists of one part varnish and six parts melted resin. A drop or two of this is rolled into a small ball between moistened fingers and placed on a stick. As specks are lifted from the varnish, they are kneaded into the ball.

The first coat of varnish (natural varnish) can be applied more easily and will bond more readily if it is first thinned with pure turpentine. This should be in a proportion of about one part turpentine to five parts varnish. The finisher starts with the surfaces which are least exposed, and, wherever possible, turns the work so that the surface on which he is working is in a horizontal position. The varnish will set after the brush has been dipped into it to about one third the length of the bristles, and then tapped lightly against a strike wire or the side of the container.

Varnish should be applied with smooth, deliberate strokes. On large

A varnish should be warmed before its application. Left for a few minutes in a pan of water heated to seventy or eighty degrees it will reach the right consistency.

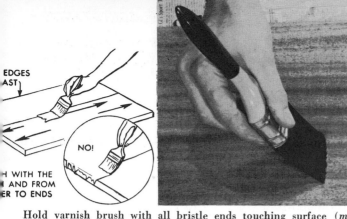

Hold varnish brush with all bristle ends touching surface (*middle*). *Right:* Lift bristles stuck in finish with brush's corner. Cover edges at end of stroke, not beginning (*left*).

flat surfaces, the brushing begins at the center and works toward the sides. In this way, the laps can be worked with less than a full brush. After the whole surface has been covered, it should be tipped off with light brush strokes which run with the grain from one end to the other.

When a finisher varnishes a framed panel, he cuts in, or coats, any molding first, then cross-brushes, and finally tips off with the grain. Cross-brushing is a useful technique for obtaining a level coat, especially when working on a vertical surface. Although it is not required on horizontal surfaces, it is good insurance against skips, or "holidays." A film of varnish is difficult to see, unless the work is placed so that the finish film can be viewed

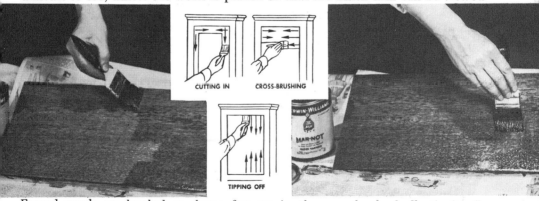

CUTTING IN   CROSS-BRUSHING

TIPPING OFF

Framed panels are brushed as above: first cut in, then cross-brush, finally tip it off.

in oblique light. This makes it easier to discover spots which otherwise may be missed. The first coat should be given plenty of time to dry. Regular varnishes require from twelve to thirty-six hours, but many of the new synthetics will set, dust-free, in an hour or less, and harden in as little as four hours.

All finishing materials must be thoroughly dry before sanding. The first coat should be sanded with 6/0 garnet paper to knock off the gloss, and special care must be taken not to cut through the film, especially at the edges. Before the second coat is applied, the surface should be dusted carefully. A tack rag is best for picking up the final traces of dust. To make one, dip a cotton handkerchief into warm water, wring out lightly, sprinkle with turpentine, and dip it in varnish. Finally, wring the cloth out until it is nearly dry. When not being used, the tack rag should be stored in an airtight container. Prepared tack rags also are available.

The second and third coats of varnish should be applied at can consistency. The procedure used for applying the first coat is followed for applying the second and third coats. When dry, the final coat should be rubbed to a satin finish. Using rubbed-effect, semi-gloss varnish instead of high-gloss varnish for the final coat is a great time-saver.

The job will be completed sooner if sanding sealer can be substituted for the first varnish coat. Sanding sealer dries to recoat in approximately an hour, brushes easily, and builds well. Its greatest advantage is that it contains a sanding agent which permits clean, powdery sanding without gumming of the abrasive.

SPIRIT VARNISHES

Spirit varnishes contain no drying oils. Instead, they harden through the evaporation of a solvent (usually alcohol or turpentine). It automatically follows that any spirit varnish is much quicker-drying than even the short-oil varnishes. The best known spirit varnish is *shellac*, a purified form of the resinous matter produced by the lac insect of India. Shellac has been a popular furniture finish for centuries, and you are quite likely to find it on any quality piece which is more than fifty years old. French polish, the favorite finish of many furniture connoisseurs, is a series of thin coats of shellac applied by painstaking hand rubbing. While shellac can be purchased in solid flake form, it is sold much more commonly as a liquid with the resin dissolved in alcohol.

Shellac is available in two different grades of refinement. The natural color of shellac is a reddish-brown. Orange shellac is made by dissolving this natural shellac gum in denatured alcohol. White shellac is a clearer liquid made by bleaching the resin before dissolving it in alcohol. Most cans of shellac are labeled "four-pound cut" or "five-pound cut," meaning that either four or five pounds of shellac gum were dissolved in one gallon of alcohol to make the mixture.

Shellac can be applied with brush or spray gun. It is almost never used without thinning. Two thin coats will wear better than one thick one, and the mixing formula generally followed is the addition of one part of denatured alcohol to two parts of the shellac as it comes from the can. The wash coats so frequently referred to should be about the consistency of water (slightly thicker for sealing filler on some woods), or about a one-to-two pound cut.

Because shellac is subject to aging, only as much as is needed for the job at hand should be purchased. Only denatured alcohol should be used for mixing and thinning. Shellac can be tinted by adding small amounts of a hand-mixed toner (dye dissolved in a solvent, in this case, alcohol). Pigmented shellac, or shellac enamel, is available in either black or white. The white is used as an undercoat for enamel, paint, or lacquer.

Shellac has certain disadvantages. It has very little resistance to heat or water; for example, a wet glass will leave a white ring on a shellac finish. It will be dissolved by alcohol, its solvent. It will also "bloom" (that is, cloud or turn white) if applied on a humid day or over a damp surface. However, this can be remedied by mixing shellac with shellac-mixing lacquer. This mixture is a crisp-drying product which combines the excellent sealing action of shellac with the water resistance and hardness of lacquer. The main disadvantage of using shellac is that it loses its drying properties in time; it becomes so gummy that it simply will not dry. This problem is avoided, however, if shellac is purchased only as needed in small cans.

White, or "clear," shellac is used for most work. It is a must for blond finishes. Orange shellac works well on darker woods. Tinted shellac is often used for toning a finish in which the stain does not turn out to be quite the right color. Such transparent toners are made by mixing alcohol-soluble, powdered stain with alcohol, and adding this tinting liquid to the shellac, as required. This same trick may be used with varnish and lacquer finishes, substituting oil-soluble and lacquer-soluble powdered stains.

To apply shellac, a soft varnish brush should be used. The solution dries quickly, and the finisher must work rapidly, using long, sweeping strokes—one stroke to apply, one stroke to tip off. Shellac which is heavier than the three-pound cut should not be used, because thin coats not only give a better finish, but also make brushing much easier. Brushing should be held to a minimum (ideally, two strokes on any surface), since excessive brushing will pile the shellac up in ridges and show laps. Between coats, shellac should be rubbed down with fine sandpaper or steel wool. The final coat can be rubbed with very fine steel wool or 2/0 pumice and rubbing oil. Shellac is not waterproof, so water should never be used as a rubbing lubricant.

REDUCTIONS FOR STANDARD SHELLAC CUTS

Operation	Cut	3-lb. Base		4-lb. Base		5-lb. Base	
		Alcohol	Shellac	Alcohol	Shellac	Alcohol	Shellac
Wash Coat	½ lb.	4	1	5	1	7	1
First Coat	1 lb.	4	3	2	1	2	1
Second Coat ..	2 lb.	2	5	3	4	1	1
Third Coat ...	3 lb.	—	—	1	4	1	2
General Use ..	2½ lb.	1	5	1	2	2	3

Alcohol and shellac proportions are given in liquid parts. For example, if with a four-pound cut shellac the finisher wants one pound for the first coat, it can be seen from the table following that this requires two parts alcohol and one part of four-pound cut shellac.

OPAQUE FINISHES

Each of the common transparent finishes, except oil and wax, has its opaque counterpart. Pigmented varnish is *enamel*; pigments ground in solvents blended with nitro-cellulose make *lacquer enamel*; *synthetic enamels* are made by grinding pigments in synthetic resin.

Unlike transparent finishes, enamel can be applied over an old finish, if the original finish is still in good condition. A finish will not adhere to an oily or waxy surface, however, and the finish is never smoother than the surface over which it is applied. Wax and oil from furniture polishes must first be washed off with a strong detergent solution. If the surface is reasonably clean, it can be wiped with turpentine, alcohol, or any of the special preparations made for cleaning and conditioning old paint. One coat of enamel will cover most surfaces, unless the old finish is in poor condition. If the old finish has been removed—and this is recommended in most cases—two coats of enamel, or one coat of undercoat and one coat of enamel should be applied.

Since enamel is a pigmented finish, it should be mixed well in order to distribute the color pigment evenly. It is better to stir the enamel with a paddle which will reach the bottom of the can than to shake the can causing troublesome bubbles.

Two-way brushing is the best method to achieve a smooth, even enamel film. The enamel should be laid on across the grain, then brushed out lightly with the grain. The finisher first covers a small area in this manner, then moves on to the next small area. As with regular varnish, lighting should be arranged so that it reflects off the wet surface. This helps to avoid skips, runs and ridging, or piling-up of the material. If a run, or sag, does occur in fresh enamel, it can be worked out with a brush which is nearly dry. Runs and sags on partly-set enamel should be worked out with a loaded brush.

If two coats of enamel are to be applied, it is usually best to thin the first coat with about 10 per cent pure turpentine, or the reducer recommended by the manufacturer. Enamel undercoat is white; this is usually satisfactory for use under light colors. If a dark-colored enamel is to be applied, it is best to tint the undercoat with the enamel (about three parts undercoat to one part enamel). Of course, oil colors also can be used to tint the undercoat.

Enamels are either high-gloss or semi-gloss. To make the high-gloss enamel only a trifle less shiny, a little semi-gloss of the same color can be added. This same result can be obtained by mixing undercoat with the gloss enamel, but the undercoat must be tinted with oil colors to match the enamel. To lighten a color, a little white enamel and a few drops of blue, ground-in-oil, tinting color are added.

It is important to sand down dead-sharp corners to a radius about that of the lead in a pencil. Such edges will still appear sharp, but will hold enamel without chipping.

Opaque finishes are useful for concealing poor grain or blemished and scarred surfaces. Some, like the opaque primer-sealer shown above, also provide undercoat for the finish.

LACQUERS

Spraying on a lacquer finish is one of the fastest and best ways of finishing furniture. *Lacquers* are quick-drying finishes consisting of nitrocellulose (cotton fiber treated with acids) and a mixture of volatile solvents, which produce a hard, durable, heat- and water-proof finish. Lacquer thinners are made by blending one or more solvents of lacquer (ethyl acetate, butyl acetate, etc.) with other non-solvent materials (denatured alcohol or benzol), which only become solvents when combined with true solvents. These thinners are generally classified according to their drying time (fast, medium, or slow). Adding the slower-drying thinners, known as retarders, makes brushing lacquer. Generally, lacquer must be applied with a spray gun because it is so fast-drying. Spray lacquers dry in minutes, which completely solves the dust problem. This alone is enough to make sprayed lacquer highly desirable.

When clear (water-white) lacquers are applied over unstained wood, they tend to lack the depth of a natural varnish. More than one or two coats may be required on some woods (especially the darker woods) in order to achieve the illusion of depth.

Lacquer solvents are very powerful, and this must be taken into consideration when filling. If lacquer is to be used as a top coat over open-grained woods, the filler must be thinned with naphtha instead of turpentine. A sanding sealer should be used on close-grained woods. Each coat of lacquer dissolves a small amount of the preceding coat, which assures a perfect bond.

Lacquer can be applied over the bare, sanded wood, but a sanding sealer is usually used for the first coat since it is about equal in build to two coats of lacquer. Sanding between coats is confined to a light once-over with 6/0 paper to knock off any dust flecks.

The use of lacquer in refinishing can present difficulties unless every bit of the old finish has been removed. The solvents in lacquer will "lift" varnish; that is, they will act as a remover. This can be remedied by using a shellac sealer or a special lacquer which is compatible with varnish to protect the old finish. Since many old finishes are difficult to identify, the above procedure should be followed in case the finish *might* be varnish. Otherwise, the old finish should be removed completely.

Brushing lacquer is becoming more popular because of its durability, water and alcohol resistance, clarity of body, ease of application and fast-drying properties. It is self-leveling, a feature appreciated by amateur and professional finishers alike. There are no brush-mark worries when applying lacquer. Brushing lacquer, as it comes from the can, is very nearly water-white and water-thin, and it flows onto a well-prepared surface as easily as shellac. "Brushing" is really the wrong term to use here; actually, you lay, or flow, a brushing lacquer or any other fast-drying finish.

The brush should be kept wet and the finish laid on with one smooth, sweeping stroke. It will flow out to form a glass-like film. Your only worry is that of always brushing to a wet edge; you have to work moderately fast. Back-and-forth brushing is out, especially on the second coat, because back sweeps of the brush will lift the coat already applied. Two coats applied over a sanding sealer usually make a satisfactory finish.

SYNTHETICS

Synthetic finishes contain synthetic, or artificial, rather than natural resins. Almost every lacquer or varnish has its synthetic counterpart. Four-hour varnishes, for instance, are synthetics. They generally dry rapidly and can be applied in thicker coats. Usually, such synthetics are applied in much the same manner as the natural-resin finish which they resemble, and thus it is impossible to give any standard method of application which holds true for all synthetics. It is important that you read the application instructions on the containers. However, there are certain groups of synthetic finishes which have no natural counterparts.

For example, *catalyst finishes* are liquid-plastic materials which are cured by means of a catalyst, or hardening agent, which is added to the material just before application. Usually sold under a trade name, these finishes are extremely hard and are proofed against almost anything—boiling water, alcohol, lacquer thinner, and even some varnish removers. Not all finishes in this group bond readily to an undercoat, and they should be applied to bare or stained wood only. Do not use a sealer or pigmented stain under a catalyst-type material.

The amount of catalyst varies with different products. Phenolin, a typical catalyst finish, takes one-and-one-half ounces of hardening agent per quart. This specific product is best applied with a spray gun, but it can be brushed. It is usually dry enough for sanding in one or two hours, but the second (and final) coat requires 24 hours for drying before rubbing down.

Many catalyst finishes, especially the alkyds, require baking in order to cure the surface film properly. Phenolic resins used with a catalyst usually are air-dry or bake type. Infra-red heat lamps can be used for baking. Usually one or two lamps will do nicely for small jobs. The resulting finish is extremely hard, tough, and durable; therefore, these synthetics should be used where such characteristics are of primary concern.

Penetrating finishes were originally developed for use on floors, the idea being that a finish which was in the wood rather than on the surface wouldn't wear or scratch. These sealer-finish materials are made in both wax-resin and resin-oil bases, and are intended to be applied to bare wood only. The wax type cannot be coated with any other type of material, but the resin-oil base can be topped with varnish.

Penetrating finishes lack the body and surface-building characteristics of varnish and lacquer, but they wear well, do not fade appreciably, and are easy to apply without sags, runs, or laps. If extra luster is desired, it can be obtained by waxing.

While less popular as indoor furniture finishes, *paints* are the most common opaque finishes. *Oil paints* are made by grinding pigments in linseed oil and thinning the mixture with a solvent, usually turpentine. A more glossy finish can be obtained by increasing the percentage of oil. *Water paints* use a synthetic binder instead of linseed oil and can be thinned with water. So-called rubber or latex paint is a special type of water paint.

The beginner is often confused by the great number of finishing products which combine two or more of these steps into one operation: for example, "staining fillers," "staining sealers," "varnish stains," and even "one-step finishes." Since he probably is not familiar with the characteristics of standard finishing materials and their methods of application, he is unable to make any reasonable comparison between these finishes and traditional finishes.

Most of these special finishes come close to duplicating the result obtained when each step is carried out as a separate operation. The obvious advantage of combination finishes is that they save time and work. Of course, few furniture restorers would consider using such a product on a valuable antique, but they usually prove satisfactory for refinishing an heirloom of lesser value.

Developments in the field of synthetics are taking place so rapidly today that it is almost impossible to give specific information which might be helpful in selecting a combination finish. The best way to learn whether any one of these will satisfy your needs is to try them on test panels. Local paint or hardware dealers will be glad to give you more information about specific brands.

Two transparent finishes which do not fit into any of the above categories are those using wax or linseed oil as finishing materials. *Wax finishes* are applied over bare wood or stain, and give a pleasing eggshell gloss which.

although durable, can be damaged by water or excessive heat. Furniture waxes are sold in three forms: paste, liquid, and cream. The latter two contain either solvents or neutral soaps and cleanse as well as polish. However, paste wax gives the most durable surface and this type is most commonly used for a straight wax finish.

Furniture waxes are made by blending a number of different kinds of wax, thereby taking advantage of the best qualities of each. For instance, carnauba, or Brazil wax, one of the hardest of all natural waxes, has a melting point of 185°. However, it is much too brittle to be used alone and, for this reason, is always combined with other waxes, such as beeswax or paraffin. *Staining waxes* are made by adding oil stain to wax. They should be used on bare wood only, with no sealer. Any furniture wax can be tinted by adding color in japan. Most waxes can be thinned or removed with turpentine. Wax finishes must be renewed periodically with additional coats.

RUBBING TECHNIQUES

Once you have applied the last finishing coat, the true finishing touch is rubbing down that final coat. Don't be overcome with the initial beauty of the handiwork, for the job still is not done. It is surprising how rough the surface feels to the touch. After the finish has been built, it is necessary to follow through with the final step. The finisher should not be satisfied with a smooth-to-the-touch surface; it must be glass-smooth, like the surface of a high-grade mirror. Rubbing the finish with lubricated abrasive removes brush marks, orange peel (the wavy effect caused by improper spraying), dust flecks, and bubbles. All of these are common defects which are almost impossible to avoid entirely unless the finish can be applied under ideal conditions of dust-free air and rigid temperature control.

The first rubbing removes defects and levels the finish, giving it a dull, flat appearance. Polishing will bring the surface to a fairly high sheen but, when rubbing antiques, many restorers prefer to leave the finish dull. Although a cloth pad can be used for rubbing, a hard felt pad is preferable. Felt has just enough "give" to follow slight irregularities without danger of cutting through the finish. Powdered pumice, of FFF grade or finer, is commonly used for the first rub-down. Pour the powder into a tumbler of water and allow it to settle before you pour off part of the water. Then mix the sediment into a creamy paste.

Some finishers prefer to use oil instead of water, since oil slows the cutting. In either case, mix the pumice and lubricant into a creamy paste and pour or brush it on the surface to be rubbed.

When rubbing with an abrasive-charged felt pad, a long, sweeping stroke should be used. The strokes should overlap by about half the width of the pad. The finisher always rubs with the grain on straight-grained woods, and the long way on panels having other grain patterns. Greater care must be

BEFORE RUBBING

AFTER RUBBING

Above right: Mix lubricant and pumice into a creamy paste, brush or pour onto surface to be rubbed. Rub with abrasive-charged felt pad. *Below:* Rubbing uses long, even strokes under moderate pressure. Diagram shows how to rub and the effects of good job—a fine, mirror-smooth, high-gloss finish.

After rubbing, the slush that accumulated should be cleaned off with wiping rag soaked in naphtha.

taken when working near edges, allowing the pad to overlap the edge only an inch or so at each stroke. It is necessary to acquire the knack of easing up on the pressure at an edge to avoid cutting through the finish and exposing a narrow line of bare wood.

The progress of the work can be checked occasionally by cleaning off the surface and examining it closely in a good light. An easy way to determine the uniformity of the surface is to look across it obliquely. Small areas which are still rough or untouched are easily spotted in this way. When the surface is uniformly flat and feels smooth to the touch of a fingertip, it is ready for the final polishing.

Turnings and decorative carvings may be rubbed with an abrasive-charged muslin cloth, but there is a danger of rubbing the finish off the high places. Small carvings can be rubbed with a discarded toothbrush after painting the surface with abrasive cream; larger carvings can often be rubbed with a worn scrubbing brush or a suede shoe brush. As a rule, carvings and the short-radius portions of turnings are left with a dull-gloss finish.

A finer abrasive is required for polishing. However, if water has been used to lubricate the FFF pumice, continued rubbing will grind this abrasive until it becomes finer and finer. Thus, one thorough rubbing with pumice will produce a medium-low sheen without a separate operation. If this is satisfactory, leave the spent rubbing slush on the surface and do the final rubbing with clean cotton waste.

For a higher sheen, let the work stand overnight and then continue the rubbing operation with rottenstone lubricated with rubbing oil. Rottenstone does not actually cut like pumice, but it will bring up a polish quickly if the work has been pumice-rubbed until it is absolutely level. After it has been rubbed, the surface should be cleaned with a damp cloth.

Lacquer presents a harder surface than varnish and is often rubbed with wet-or-dry abrasive papers which cut much faster than pumice. Even if the softer action of pumice is preferred, a quick cut-down with 8/0 paper, lubricated with water or oil, will greatly lessen the labor of pumice rubbing. A satisfactory satin finish can be obtained with 8/0 paper or very fine steel wool alone; this can be followed by rottenstone polish if a higher gloss is desired.

Commercial rubbing compounds are available in a variety of types and grits for coarse or fine polishing. These come in paste form, and are used with or without a lubricant, depending on the type. Many finishers prefer them to the older pumice and rottenstone abrasives.

The following is a descriptive listing of the various rubbing materials needed:

Rubbing Felt—A soft, pressed felt, measuring approximately three by five inches, and at least one-half inch thick, and several smaller pieces.

Abrasive Paper—6/0 (220-grit), 8/0 (280), and 9/0 (320) wet-or-dry silicon carbide.

Pumice—No. 1 for coarse rubbing, and nos. FF or FFF for fine rubbing.

Rottenstone—For fine rubbing.

Rubbing Oil—Lubricant for rubbing, which is purchased ready-mixed. Paraffin oil, crude petroleum, or light motor oil thinned with benzine can be used.

Naphtha—For cleaning up rubbing slush.

Polishing Oil—Purchased ready-mixed. A homemade mix can be made with half olive oil and half alcohol. Standard household furniture polishes can be used.

White Soap—Any white soap which is used to keep fine abrasive paper from loading.

Rubbing Compound—Ready-mixed paste or liquid abrasive, available in various grades of fineness.

Lacquer Polish—For cleaning up rubbing compound haze; a large number of ready-mixed products available. Automatic polish can be used.

Alcohol—Used to spirit-off polishing oil. Add water as necessary to reduce strength.

WAX FINISHES

Not much pure technique is involved in applying a *wax finish*. First, a thin coat of shellac, varnish, or lacquer is applied. After this has dried, it is rubbed down with steel wool; then an even coat of paste wax is applied with a cloth. When this is dry (in from 10 minutes to an hour), it should be rubbed briskly with a soft cloth. At least two coats of wax are required for a good finish. This should be renewed periodically with additional coats.

Preparation of the various waxes needed for finishing is as follows:

Hard—Carnauba wax, one-pound; caresine wax, one-pound; turpentine, one pint. Shred the waxes into a can and put the can in boiling water over a flame. After the wax melts, remove from heat and add the turpentine, which should be warmed in hot water; *never warm it over open flame.*

Medium Hard—White or yellow beeswax, one-pound; turpentine, one-half pint. Mix by heating as above, or shred wax in turpentine and let stand overnight.

Colored—Mix the turpentine in the above formulas with a small amount of the desired color in japan. Burnt umber or Van Dyke brown are satisfactory for browns; Venetian red makes a good red wax. Dry color can be used for ready-mixed wax. Dry burnt umber makes a good brown wax; use about a teaspoonful of color per pound of wax.

Antique White—To one pint of liquid wax, add about one ounce of powdered rottenstone or dry sienna. Shred and melt paraffin wax. Thin as

powdered rottenstone or dry sienna. Shred and melt paraffin wax. Thin as desired with a fifty-fifty mix of turpentine and naphtha. Color with a little dry zinc white.

This synthetic finish is very simple to apply. Merely wipe finish on the surface with a lint-free cloth, rubbing with the grain. Of course it is necessary to carefully prevent runs and drips, but this finish should be applied freely. As soon as the first coat of finish is dry (about twenty-four hours later), the surface is ready to be rubbed with an abrasive paper. This job should use superfine, wet-or-dry abrasive.

To lubricate the abrasive, mix a few flakes of mild soap in warm water, and apply this to the finish with a sponge or cloth. Sand the surface using just enough pressure to bring out sheen, but avoid going completely through the finish.

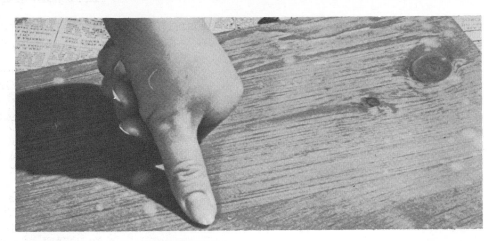

By wiping surface with a finger, check progress of sanding continually. Wipe surface with a soft cloth when looks uniformly dull. Touch up carefully, using an artist's brush.

Apply a second coat and sand it down. Rub surface lightly with 4/0 steel wool until it is perfectly smooth in looks and feel. Then wipe it off with a soft clean cloth.

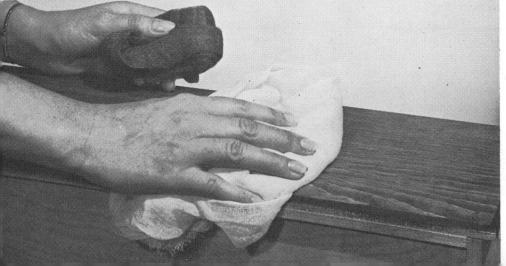

OIL FINISHES

A hand-rubbed *oil finish* has to be a labor of love. Because approximately the same effect can be achieved with a penetrating finish, only a perfectionist, purist, or someone who simply enjoys work is likely to decide on an oil finish. In case you happen to belong in any of these three categories, here's how it's done:

Few materials or tools are needed. The oil used for a hand-rubbed oil finish is pure, boiled linseed oil. Raw linseed oil is thin, dark, and slow-drying. Formerly, this was allowed to season for several years in the sun so that it would become clearer, heavier-bodied, and tacky. Linseed oil seasoned in this way is, or was, known as "stand oil." A short cut for making stand oil is by kettle-boiling, which thickens the oil by means of the direct application of heat.

Today, pure linseed oil is reinforced by the addition of polymerized or heat-treated linseed oil, plus driers. This product has all the toughness of the raw oil film. It is faster drying, and should be used wherever an oil finish is indicated.

Although most rubbing is done with the heel of the hand, the time-honored material for final rubbing of an oil finish is mule hide. However, other leathers, canvas, or cloth will all produce acceptable results. The only two tools needed are a buffing stick and a buffing block, both of which should be surfaced with some rubbing material. A wood block faced with leather is often preferred. The surface must be perfectly smooth before applying the oil. It is best to raise the grain with water and sand down first.

A number of different procedures are used in applying oil. The simplest, but also the most tedious, is the application of straight coats of boiled linseed oil. Each coat is applied with a cloth or brush and immediately rubbed into the wood with the heel of the hand. More oil is added until it stands out on the surface; and rubbing is continued until the surface oil disappears. Oil is never left to dry on the surface. Rubbed oil finishes have always been popular for gunstocks, and the gunsmith's rule used to be: rub once a day for a week, once a week for a month, once a month for a year, and once a year for life.

The pores of open-grain wood are often filled with paste filler before applying oil, or over a single coat of raw linseed oil, which acts as a staining medium. This filler will lessen the absorptive action of the bare wood, and allow oil coats to build faster with somewhat less labor. The surface is sanded with 8/0 paper, as needed during the rubbing.

Another method is to start with a coat of raw linseed oil mixed with turpentine (three parts oil to one part turpentine), letting this stand for thirty minutes, then wiping clean and leaving it overnight. Next, paste filler is applied and allowed to dry for twenty-four hours. Then begins the "once a day for a week," rule, using boiled linseed oil. Before the fourth rubbing, it is sanded with 8/0 garnet paper; before the seventh rubbing, 3/0 steel wool is used. For the eighth rubbing, half-and-half japan drier is added to the linseed oil. This coat is let stand until it becomes tacky; then it is rubbed with burlap or some other coarse material. The pores of the wood should be inspected. If they are not filled nearly level, thinned paste filler should be applied.

The final rubbing stage has been reached. A little rottenstone is now applied to the rubbing surface of the buffing stick and buffing block. The block is used for flat surfaces and the stick is used as a file. This step will remove any gummy oil deposits on the surface of the work. The leather will become slick and shiny from the oil it picks up and should be scraped clean with a knife.

After the surface has been rubbed with rottenstone, additional coats of oil mixed with turpentine (three to one, as before) are applied. This mixture makes a good furniture polish for any surface, and should be applied periodically, following the old gunsmith's formula.

A method of oil finishing that once found favor with finishers, which has been now largely displaced, is that of applying oil to the surface and then rubbing it down with a fine steel-wool pad. In this method, the pad is rinsed occasionally and the process continued. On open-grain woods the sludge formed by this process serves as a filler. Gunstocks have been finished by this method, with the oil being tinted lightly by the addition of Venetian or French red. Like wax finishes, oil finishes must be periodically renewed.

SPECIAL FINISHING EFFECTS

A number of *special finishing effects* can be obtained by selective spraying or wiping to darken or lighten certain areas of the work so that they will be in contrast to the general tone of the piece. Most such effects simulate the effects of wear or age. These effects are:

Shading, or darkening some areas, which is usually done with a spray gun by using a stain or a prepared toner. The simplest way of achieving a shaded effect is to spray lightly on some parts and heavier on others when applying the stain. Another method of stain-shading is to apply a coat of diluted stain first, allow it to dry, and shade certain areas with the second coat of stain. There are two types of shading. In sharp-shading, which is largely confined to colored enamels, the color separation is strong and clearly defined. Soft-shading, on the other hand, is done by feathering one color over another, usually a dark color over a lighter one. Shading may be added at any point in the finishing schedule. Special shading stains can be purchased ready-mixed, or they can be made by mixing powder stain with thin shellac or lacquer.

Highlighting is the reverse of shading—instead of certain areas being darkened, others are lightened. This is easy to do with pigmented oil stain, and is practical with almost any other type of stain. Cleaner wiping for highlights can be obtained if a second highlighting coat of pigmented stain is applied over a sealer. Highlighting can also be done mechanically after the first stain coat is dry by using fine sandpaper or steel wool to lighten certain areas. However, care must be taken not to cut entirely through the under-coats because restaining to match may prove rather difficult.

Glazing most nearly describes the whole art of using a wiped, translucent shading medium. A piece of work can be glazed and then wiped for high-lights, or a glaze coat can be used for a textured ground, or to imitate wood

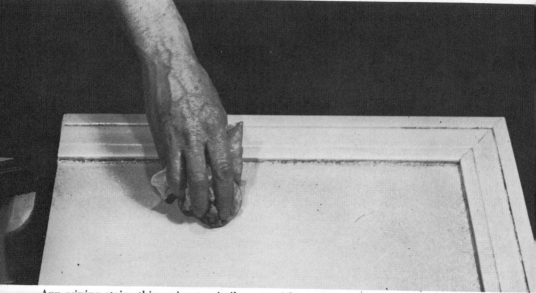

Any wiping stain, thin paint or similar material can be used for glazing; but usually a specially prepared "glazing liquid," which is easily made or readily purchased, is used.

grain. The glaze itself can be any wiping stain, thin paint, or similar mate-rial, but usually a specially prepared product called "glazing liquid" is used. This can be purchased ready-mixed or made by blending varnish (four parts), boiled linseed oil (two parts), and turpentine (one part). Pigment colors in oil or japan are added as needed to obtain desired tints.

One traditional antique finish is a two-tone blended, or shaded, finish achieved by applying a coat of tinted glazing liquid over an enamel base coat. Usually, the glaze is applied over white or ivory enamel, but an infinite num-ber of antique effects are possible by using other colors.

The glaze coat is applied over a foundation coat of sealer or colored enamel. It is sprayed or brushed over the whole area and immediately wiped with a cloth or blended out with a dry brush. It may also be applied with a cloth and then wiped with the same cloth in a kind of rubbing-on process.

A soft, brown glaze on an off-white enamel ground, such as bone-white or ivory, is very effective on some pieces. The same glaze on a cream ground gives a pleasant, warm effect. For a clear finish, the glaze coat should be somewhat darker than the wood or than the stained color of the wood. For

HIGHLIGHT BULBOUS PORTIONS OF TURNING

NATURAL HIGHLIGHT CAUSED BY WEAR

HIGHLIGHT IMITATING WEAR

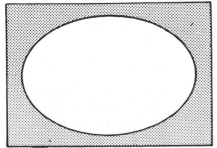

CORRECT—NARROW RIM OF DARKER COLOR

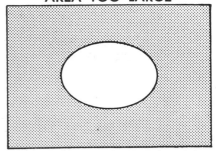

INCORRECT—SHADED AREA TOO LARGE

colored enamel finishes, any of hundreds of color combinations can be used.

The glaze should be wiped thoroughly for most work. Graining effects can be obtained by wiping the glaze coat with a dry brush, whisk broom, or a textured fabric. If the glazing coat becomes too tacky for clean working, it can be softened by wiping lightly with a cloth moistened with naphtha.

Regardless of the technique used, it should not be overdone. On clear finishes especially, any shading or highlighting should be soft. A combination of methods is often useful; for instance, it is nearly impossible to spray-shade carvings, but it is very easy to apply pigment stain or glaze and then expose the highlights by wiping. On the other hand, the spray gun does a perfect job of shading panels and table tops. Turnings are shaded best by wiping because a simple wiping with a rag from one end to the other will automatically highlight any bulbous portions.

VI

Schedules for Finishing

Whole books are devoted to nothing but the subject of finishing schedules, because there are literally hundreds of different ones. Nevertheless, all of the schedules for common finishes are included here. Local libraries can provide more detailed information for schedules covering such items as novelty finishes. Most paint manufacturers will also supply schedules for their specific products.

BASIC SCHEDULES

Open-grain wood—Brushing or spraying, single-stain system, for oak, walnut, mahogany, and other open-grain woods:

> 1. Brush or spray NGR stain of desired color. Dry twenty-thirty minutes.
> 2. Brush or spray wash-coat of lacquer or white shellac. Dry ten minutes.
> 3. Sand with 6/0 garnet; dry and dust off.
> 4. Fill with paste wood filler of desired color. Dry from thirty minutes to twenty-four hours, depending on product used.
> 5. Brush or spray wet coat of sanding sealer. Dry one hour.
> 6. Sand with 6/0 garnet; dry and dust.
> 7. Apply second coat of sealer. Sand as before.
> 8. Spray two coats of clear gloss lacquer, or brush one coat of varnish. Lacquer should dry overnight, varnish at least twenty-hour hours before rubbing.
> 9. Rub to satin finish with rubbing compound applied with burlap pad.

NOTE: Rubbing can be eliminated by using final top coat of rubbed-effect varnish or lacquer. Step No. 2 can be omitted if desired.

Open-grain wood—Brushing or spraying, double-stain system:

1. Brush or spray NGR stain. Dry twenty minutes.
2. Fill with paste wood filler. Dry as required.
3. Apply first coat of sanding sealer. Dry one hour.
4. Sand with 6/0 garnet.
5. Apply second coat of sealer. Dry and sand.
6. Brush or spray wet coat of pigment wiping stain, the color of which should be a little darker than NGR. Let stand two to ten minutes as needed; wipe with a soft cloth, wiping clean or shading as desired. Dry thirty minutes.
7. Apply top coats of varnish or lacquer.

NOTE: Double staining is recommended for off-color wood, also for shaded and antiqued effects. Shading can also be done by spraying NGR stain or shading stain. The wiping stain is recommended for the brush system.

Close-grain wood—Lacquer system for birch, maple, and other close-grain woods:

1. Stain with NGR stain. Dry twenty-thirty minutes.
2. Spray lacquer sanding sealer. Dry one hour.
3. Sand with 6/0 garnet; dry and dust.
4. Apply one to three coats of clear-gloss lacquer, scuff-sanding between coats with 6/0 garnet. Let final coat dry overnight.
5. Rub (see rubbing schedules).

Close-grain wood—Brushing or spraying, double stain:

1. Brush or spray NGR stain; dry thirty minutes. Sand with 6/0.
2. Brush or spray pigment wiping stain of same color. Wipe clean or shade as desired. Dry thirty minutes.
3. Brush or spray sanding sealer. Dry one hour.
4. Sand with 6/0 garnet; dry and dust.
5. Apply two coats of lacquer or one coat of varnish.
6. Rub.

NOTE: For quality work, more coats of top material can be used to get a thicker film for thorough rubbing and a high-luster finish.

Close-grain wood—Spray only, double-stain system:

1. Spray pigment wiping stain. Wipe clean with rag. Dry thirty minutes.
2. Thin same stain one part to three parts naphtha. Spray-shade the work. Do not wipe. Dry thirty minutes.
3. Finish with sealer and top coats.

NOTE: Although this is similar to the preceding schedules, there is a change in stain and application.

Close-grain wood—Brush or spray, double stain. (This gives a nice tone on maple, poplar, birch, or pine) :

1. Brush or spray pigment wiping stain of desired color. Let dry until it start to flat, then wipe with rag. Dry thirty minutes.
2. Brush or spray sanding sealer. Dry one hour.
3. Sand with 6/0 garnet. Use 3/0 steel wool for moldings and carvings. Dust.
4. The application of a second coat of sealer is optional. Sand as before.
5. Brush or spray pigment wiping stain, as in Step 1.
6. Varnish or lacquer top coats as desired.

NOTE: The second staining operation can be omitted if desired.

Uniforming Schedule—For finishing open- and close-grain wood in same piece:

1. Spray or brush NGR stain or desired color. Dry thirty minutes.
2. Apply paste wood filler to all open-grain wood and to end-grain only of the close-grain wood. Wipe and let dry.
3. Brush or spray pigment wiping stain of matching color on close-grain wood only. Dry thirty minutes.
4. Brush or spray sanding sealer. Let dry one hour.
5. Sand with 6/0 garnet.
6. Repeat Steps 4 and 5.
7. Spray or brush pigment wiping stain over the entire piece, wiping and blending with rag as needed for color value. Dry thirty minutes.
7. *Alternate:* Spray shading stain or diluted wiping stain to uniform the wood. Do not wipe. Dry thirty minutes.
8. Apply top coats of varnish or lacquer.

Uniforming Schedule:

1. Apply NGR stain to light sapwood. Wipe with cloth dampened with alcohol to match color. Dry ten minutes.
2. Spray NGR stain but not wet; spray lightly on dark wood, heavy on light wood. Dry thirty minutes.
3. Spray lacquer wash coat over all.
4. Sand lightly with 6/0 garnet. Dust.
5. Fill all open-grain wood with paste wood filler.
6. Reduce same filler, one part filler to two parts naphtha. Apply to close-grain wood. Wipe off and let dry.
7. Spray wet coat sanding sealer. Dry one hour.
8. If further color toning or shading is required, spray-shading stain or thin pigment wiping stain.
9. Top coats.

LIGHT TONES

Surface Coloring System—Spray system for select white wood:

> 1. Spray uniform coat of blond lacquer.
> 2. Spray two coats of water-white lacquer.

NOTE: This can be used for other colors, such as gray, cream, or green. A tan or gray may be used on dark woods.

Surface Coloring System—Brush system for maple or birch:

> 1. Brush light-color pigment wiping stain (blond, platinum, pale birch, beechwood, or wheat). Allow to dry until tacky and then wipe clean with soft cloth. Dry thirty minutes to two hours as required.
> 2. Top coats of varnish.
> 2. *Alternate:* One coat of two-pound cut white shellac, followed by coat of paste wax.

NOTE: After the wood is colored, any top finish can be used. Water-white top coats are preferable since they retain pure tone of stain.

Stain System—Attractive light tones can be obtained on select white wood by stain; however, the wood cannot be made any lighter than its natural color:

> 1. Spray or brush diluted NGR stain of desired color. Yellow, pink and green tones are practical. Dry thirty minutes.
> 2. Finish with any of first four basic schedules.

Bleach System (open-grain wood)—A two-solution commercial bleach gives positive light tones on most woods and provides the proper ground for attractive blond finishes:

> 1. Mix one part of No. 1 bleach with two parts No. 2. Apply with rubber sponge. Bleaching is complete in one hour but work should dry in twelve hours.
> 2. Sand lightly with 6/0 garnet. Dust.
> 3. Apply paste wood filler. Wipe and dry.
> 4. Finish with sealer; sand; apply top coats; rub.

NOTE: Color in this system is obtained entirely from the filler. Use natural filler for lightest finish; tint natural filler with oil color or oil stain for other colors.

Bleach System (open-grain wood)—Alternate Method:

> 1. Bleach the wood.
> 2. Brush or spray diluted NGR stain. (This can be pink, light green, yellow, etc.)

3. Wash coat of shellac. Dry thirty minutes.

4. Apply filler. Use natural or tint with oil color to approximate color or stain.

5. Apply top coats.

NOTE: Color in this system is obtained from the stain. Always use a wash coat, Step 3, to prevent excessive darkening from filler oils.

Bleach System (close-grain wood):

1. Bleach the wood. Let dry.

2. Sand lightly with 6/0 garnet. Dust.

3. Brush or spray desired color wiping stain (wheat, toast, suntan, platinum, champagne, etc.). Let stand until stain begins to flat, then wipe clean with soft rag.

4. Brush or spray sanding sealer, preferably water-white. Dry one hour.

5. Sand with 6/0 garnet, dry. Dust.

6. Spray two coats water-white lacquer or brush one coat clear synthetic.

7. Rub.

NOTE: After bleaching the wood, it can be finished by following any schedule for close-grain wood.

VARIOUS MATERIALS

Straight Shellac:

1. Brush or spray one-pound cut white shellac. Dry thirty minutes and scuff-sand with 6/0 garnet.

2. Apply second shellac coat, two-pound cut. Dry two-three hours and sand with 6/0 garnet.

3. Apply final shellac coat, two- or three-pound cut. Allow three hours to dry.

NOTE: For two-coat work, omit Step 1.

Shellac and Wax:

1. Apply one or two coats of shellac according to above schedule.

2. Place a small quantity of paste wax inside double thickness of cheesecloth. Apply even coat. Dry ten-fifteen minutes.

3. Rub briskly with clean cheesecloth pad. Use rotary motion; finish with long strokes. Dry one hour or more.

4. Repeat Steps 2 and 3.

NOTE: Wax finish can also be used over lacquer or varnish. For a dull finish, wipe final wax coat with a damp rag.

Penetrating Floor Sealer—A simple in-the-wood finish of maximum durability, low gloss:

> 1. Apply wet coat of penetrating floor sealer with brush or cloth. Let dry fifteen minutes and wipe off excess. Dry one hour.
> 2. Buff the surface with No. 0 steel wool.
> 3. Apply second coat. Allow ten minutes for penetration. Wipe off excess. Dry overnight.
> 4. Buff with No. 0 steel wool.
> 5. Wax.

NOTE: Penetrating floor sealers are available in resin and resin-wax types. Exact application procedure varies, and the manufacturer's directions should be followed. Most clear finishes can be colored with oil stain; some products are supplied ready-mixed in a variety of colors.

Urea-Alkyd (*catalyst finish*)—An extremely hard and durable finish for table and bar tops:

> 1. Stain with NGR stain if color is desired. Do not use pigmented stain as the adhesion is not good on undercoats of any kind.
> 2. Mix urea-alkyd synthetic with required amount of catalyst (about one-and-a-half ounces per quart), and apply with brush or spray. Dry one hour.
> 3. Sand with 6/0 garnet. Dust.
> 4. Apply second coat urea-alkyd. Dry overnight.
> 5. Rub and polish.

NOTE: Some urea-alkyd finishes require baking. The above is for air-dry or bake type. Mixed solution must be used within four hours.

Salad-Bowl Finish—A wax-resin finish for salad bowls and other turned woodenware which must resist water and various vegetable oils:

> 1. Spray impregnating salad-bowl sealer on wood. Dry one hour.
> 2. Scuff-sand with 6/0 garnet.
> 3. Spray one or two coats of salad-bowl lacquer.

NOTE: This is a lacquer system and must be sprayed. A brushing top coat is also available which makes a satisfactory finish in two coats without the impregnating sealer.

Oil Finish—A fast oil finish for guns:

> 1. De-whisker the wood by wiping with a damp cloth and drying quickly. An electric heater is ideal for this purpose. After the wood is dry, cut the whiskers with 2/0 steel wool.
> 2. Fill with natural paste wood filler, mixed and wiped the same as for finishing walnut furniture. Dry twenty-four hours.
> 3. Apply a first coat of boiled linseed oil (four parts) and spar varnish (one part). Rub with hand or cloth until dry. Let stand

forty-eight hours.

4. Apply boiled linseed oil and rub in as much as the wood is able to absorb. Polish with soft cloth until the wood is dry. Let stand a day or longer and repeat oiling until the finish is satisfactory.

NOTE: Use of filler and first coat of part varnish gives a quick build; as few as four coats of oil will bring up a good polish.

SPECIFIC WOODS

Limed Oak—A popular novelty finish for oak or chestnut showing white pores on a gray ground:

1. Bleach the wood and stain with NGR silver-gray stain. On select white oak, bleaching can be omitted.

1. *Alternate:* Spray a coat of thin gray lacquer on the wood. Easier than bleaching, this method is equally good.

2. Wash coat of shellac or lacquer only if the wood has been stained; lacquer toner provides its own seal.

3. Fill with white paste wood filler. White wiping stain can also be used although it does not have the pore-leveling effect of filler.

4. Finish with top coats of clear shellac, water-white lacquer or water-white synthetic.

5. Wax (optional).

NOTE: Be sure work is sanded perfectly smooth since even fine scratches will pick up the filler.

Ebonized Oak:

1. Spray diluted black lacquer on bare wood, just enough to get desired color.

2. Fill pores with white filler or white pigment wiping stain.

3. Apply top coats.

NOTE: Ebonized oak is the same as limed oak but has a different color ground; numerous color combinations are possible.

Ebony on Apple, Pear, or Maple:

1. Stain with hot, concentrated black NGR stain. Let dry and repeat.

2. Scuff-sand with 6/0 garnet.

3. Apply one or two top coats of any clear finishing material.

3. *Alternate:* Finish with black polishing wax (see shellac and wax schedule).

NOTE: See schedule for Ebony Black.

Cedar (Aromatic Red Cedar):

      1. Spray two-pound cut pure white shellac. Dry two hours.
      2. Rub down with 2/0 steel wool.
      3. Apply second coat of shellac, three-pound cut.
      4. Sand with 6/0 garnet or 3/0 steel wool.
      5. Apply top coat of clear gloss varnish.
      5. *Alternate:* Apply top coat of three-pound cut shellac. Rub with 3/0 steel wool and then apply furniture wax.

NOTE: Straight shellac schedule can also be used. Shellac is essential as a first coat to seal the oil in cedar. When used for closets, box interiors, etc., the wood is not finished.

Beechwood Fir—A subdued-grain finish for Douglas fir, white or yellow pine, and similar woods:

      1. Brush or spray clear plywood sealer. Let dry four hours.
      2. Scuff-sand with 6/0 garnet.
      3. Apply brush coat of beechwood (light gray-green) stain, pigmented type. Let stain dry five-ten minutes. Wipe clean with cheesecloth. Allow it to dry overnight.
      4. Apply top coats of varnish or lacquer.

NOTE: Both the sealer and pigmented stain help to subdue the grain. After coat of plywood sealer, the wood can be finished with any schedule for close-grain woods. If NGR stain is to be used, reduce the priming sealer coat with 25 per cent turpentine.

Old-World Walnut—An open-pore finish suitable for walnut, mahogany, or oak:

      1. Stain the wood medium to dark brown, using pigment oil stain. Let stain dry five minutes and then dry-brush, wiping brush occasionally on cheesecloth to remove excess stain. Then, with clean cheesecloth pad, wipe centers of panels clean, blending stain to darken at edges. Let dry overnight. Do not sand.
      2. Brush or spray sanding sealer. Dry one hour.
      3. Scuff-sand with 6/0 garnet.
      4. Apply top coat of lacquer or varnish.
      5. Rub with 3/0 steel wool.
      6. Wax with dark mineral wax.

NOTE: Feature of the above schedule is that all shading and color is obtained by dry-brushing and wiping the single coat of pigment stain. A wash coat of shellac or plywood sealer can be used as a primer if desired and will facilitate smooth blending of stain coat.

Pickled Pine:

      1. Stain with NGR gray stain for pine.

2. Brush or spray sanding sealer or two-pound cut white shellac.
3. Brush over-all coat of white pigment wiping stain. This can be wiped clean or streak-glazed with a dry brush. Another treatment is to wipe the stain across the grain, producing a smoked effect.
4. Brush or spray two-pound cut white shellac or clear synthetic.
5. *Optional:* Rub down with 3/0 steel wool and apply coat of liquid wax.

NOTE: The true pickled finish is a gray finish with an overcast of white, like the tone acquired by pickle vats. The finest work is done by first bleaching the wood. Gray stain for pine then produces an even color.

ENAMEL FINISHES

Lacquer or Synthetic Enamel:

1. Spray mist-coat lacquer enamel.
2. Sand back to bare wood with 6/0 garnet.
3. Apply two or more coats of enamel, scuff-sanding between with 6/0 garnet.

Enamel with Undercoat:

1. Wash coat of shellac. Dry twenty minutes.
1. *Alternate:* Mop, brush, or spray plywood sealer thinned one part turpentine to three parts sealer. Dry one hour.
2. Scuff-sand with 6/0 garnet. Dust.
3. Brush or spray undercoater. Spray lightly or brush out well. Dry as required.
4. Apply full wet coat of undercoater.
5. Patch. Use water putty, lacquer putty, thickened undercoater, or other suitable patching material.
6. Brush or spray first enamel coat. Scuff-sand with 6/0 garnet when dry.
7. Apply second enamel coat.
8. *Optional:* Spray only. Apply finish coat of water-white clear lacquer, or regular clear with a small amount of enamel added.
9. *Optional:* Rub down with 8/0 (280) silicon carbide with water, followed by rubbing compound for high-gloss finish.

NOTE: This schedule applies generally to lacquer, synthetic, or oil enamel. Undercoater in Step 4 may be tinted with the enamel color if desired, using 25 to 50 per cent enamel. One coat of white undercoater and one coat of enamel will usually make a satisfactory finish.

Ebony Black—A combined stain and enamel schedule for a permanent gloss black:

1. Stain with black NGR stain.

2. Fill pores with black paste wood filler. The filler used for red mahogany is satisfactory.

3. Apply two coats of black lacquer.

4. Apply two coats of water-white lacquer.

5. Rub and polish to high gloss.

NOTE: On close-grain wood, the filling operation is not required.

RUBBING SCHEDULES

Dull Satin:

1. Rub with 3/0 steel wool.
2. Polish with dry cloth.

NOTE: This rub will cut gloss quickly but will not level the surface.

Satin:

1. Rub with FF pumice and water, using felt pad. Flush with water.
2. Rub with rottenstone and water or rottenstone and rubbing oil.
3. Use wax or furniture polish, if desired.

NOTE: When finish consists of sealer, first varnish coat, and second varnish coat, the second coat can be rubbed with 320-grit wet-or-dry paper with water lubricant. The idea is to build a level surface before the top coat is applied.

Satin—Alternate Method:

1. Rub with 280- or 320-grit wet-or-dry paper with soapy water lubricant. Soap can also be applied to paper to prevent gumming. Use felt backing block to assure level surface.
2. Wipe surface with cloth and continue rubbing with 3/0 or 4/0 steel wool.
3. Apply coat of liquid wax and rub dry.

NOTE: This schedule is especially good for lacquer rubbing, either clear or pigmented.

Satin-to-Polish:

1. Rub with ready-mixed rubbing compound. Use burlap pad.
2. Clean up and wax.

NOTE: A satin-to-polish finish is produced depending on the grade of rubbing compound used. This is as fast as a steel wool rub and has more gloss. About ten strokes bring up a satin polish.

High Polish:

1. Follow any satin schedule. Let dry twelve to twenty-four hours.
2. Rub with polishing oil.

3. Remove excess oil with rag dampened with alcohol. Polish with dry cloth.

High Polish—Alternate Method:

1. Follow any satin schedule.
2. Rub with a polishing compound or automobile polish.

NOTE: Numerous rubbing and polishing compounds are available.

French Polish (*high gloss*):

1. Apply any finish with lacquer, shellac, enamel or varnish.
2. Sand with 6/0 garnet. Dust.
3. Dilute ready-mixed French polish with about 25 per cent of special solvent provided. Apply mixture to cloth pad and flatten pad on palm of hand. Pad the work with circular strokes and then finish with the grain.

NOTE: Use only improved French polish such as Qualasole, which requires no lubricant.

VII

That Professional Look

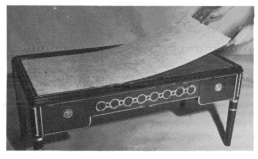
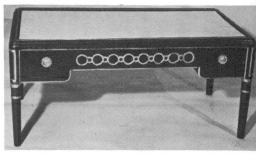

Before refinishing can be fully satisfying, and perhaps before it can even prove profitable, the novice must have acquired the touch of the professional. The following special sections explain the repairing and touching-up of difficult pieces, as well as several unusual refinishing techniques.

REPAIR OF ANTIQUES

It is often difficult to judge just how far to go in the repair and refinishing of a valuable antique. It may prove just as much a problem to decide how to refinish a later period piece or a copy you have made yourself. The condition, kind of wood, and type of finish desired are the only guides. If

131

the piece is old, it can look rather hopeless, yet it can often be brought back to its original beauty simply by washing and a spot repairing of the original finish. With genuine antiques, a complete refinishing treatment can destroy many of the valuable characteristics of age. This is also true of later period pieces to a varying extent.

It is safer when restoring an antique to proceed on the assumption that the minimum amount of change is always best. If the wood itself appears to be in reasonably good shape, and there are no bad scratches or deep dents, possibly it is only necessary to remove the old top coat and replace it with a new one. It must always be kept in mind that the more the finisher tries to make an antique look new, the less it looks like an antique. This may seem obvious, but many beginners in the art of restoring become so enthusiastic in their work that they make an antique look like a current reproduction, or copy, and thus greatly lessen its value. If at all possible, surface patina, which comes only with age, should not be disturbed. Because it can not be reproduced with any ordinary refinishing procedure, it is important to protect it. And every single small dent, scratch, or sign of wear should not be patched or repaired—these are the features which make an antique valuable.

The piece should be given a thorough going-over to decide beforehand what measures are really necessary. If there is any doubt, the more simple restoration techniques described in this chapter should be tried. If these fail to produce what the piece needs, all that is lost is a little time and no harm will have been done. If the old finish is successfully revived, a great deal of work will have been saved, and an undoubtedly more pleasing result will have been achieved.

REVIVING OLD FINISHES

Often an old finish dulled with age can be brought back to life by giving it a soap-and-water scrubbing to remove traces of old wax and imbedded dirt. If the finish under this accumulation is in reasonably good shape, possibly all that is needed is a brisk rubbing with quality furniture polish. A good washing solution for old varnishes can be made by mixing one tablespoon of turpentine, three tablespoons of boiled linseed oil, and one quart of hot water. This should be used hot (keep the container in a pan of hot water).

Before attempting to repair an old finish, try to determine what type of finish it is by testing it with different solvents in an inconspicuous spot. If alcohol softens the finish quickly, it is probably shellac. Pure turpentine usually softens or dulls old varnishes and paints. Lacquer thinner will soften some old lacquers, but some very old Chinese lacquers are not affected by modern lacquer thinners.

Clouded, transparent finishes can often be restored by rubbing with lubricated abrasive powders or with fine steel wool to remove discolored layers. Many refinishers use lemon oil instead of linseed oil for such rubbing.

Once the clouded layer has been rubbed off and cleaned up thoroughly, a small area should be tested with a new top coat. If it brightens the old finish satisfactorily, then it usually is safe to proceed and to cover all the surfaces. If not, the rubbing down is continued with occasional testing until results appear to fulfill expectations.

If there is only superficial damage to the old finish—light scratches which do not reach the wood, water marks, and checking—a liquid called an *amalgamator*, which can be obtained from any well-stocked paint supply store, can do wonders in renewing the finish. Before this is applied, the surface should be scrubbed with a mild soap to remove all dirt from the surface checks and small cracks. Amalgamator softens the old varnish or enamel, causing it to flow and level itself before hardening again. This liquid must be applied like thin varnish (the application instructions on the container should be noted in detail), and, after the surface has dried, it should be treated as if it were a new varnish finish.

Ideally, small scratches in the finish (not the wood) should be touched up with the same finishing material applied with an artist's brush or a toothpick, and then rubbed with pumice. However, several simpler short-cut materials in stick form can be used to conceal small scratches that an amalgamator will not completely conceal. Some refinishers even make use of iodine, mercurochrome, and colored crayon.

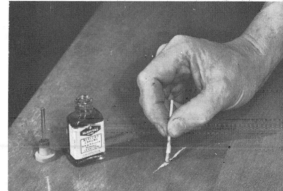

Small scratches can be patched in several ways. When colors match, shoe polish (*left*), and mercurochrome applied with a match stick tipped with cotton are probably easiest.

MAJOR REPAIRS

On the other hand, when repairs form part of the regular refinishing schedule, loose joints, cracks, and other major defects should be tackled before the old finish is removed so that the old finish will protect adjacent areas. Surface blemishes (deep scratches, dents, and rough spots) should be repaired after the old finish has been removed, allowing you to give repaired portions the same treatment as the rest of the surface, thus avoiding blending problems.

Refinishing which involves major restoration is sometimes so elaborate that it almost amounts to building a copy of the original piece of furniture. The piece should be taken apart, so that each member can be repaired and sanded separately. Broken chair rungs or legs are either doweled, reglued or, if they are beyond repair, replaced with new members. After sanding and repair, the parts are reassembled using modern adhesives, and the whole piece treated as a new finishing job.

Epoxy will fix loose rungs quite well. Joints or grooves if replacing panels on drawers can be cut out with a router, as *right*. A shaper cuts decorative grooves in replacement panels for chair backs, cut from flat stock with saber saw (*below right, left*).

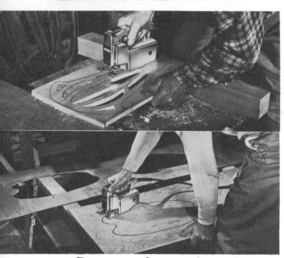

Deep scratches, cracks, and gouges are commonly filled with stick shellac which either matches or is a little darker than the original color. In the case of cigarette burns which go through the finish, all traces of charred wood must be scraped away before filling. Stick shellac is available in many colors, so matching is not usually a problem. The shellac is melted directly from the stick into the depression, then sanded flush with the adjacent surface. If the scars are very deep, they can be partially filled with wood putty before they are filled with stick shellac. A repair kit is marketed which consists of a tube of wood filler and four wax stains in crayon form. By blending the stain colors, almost any old finish can be matched.

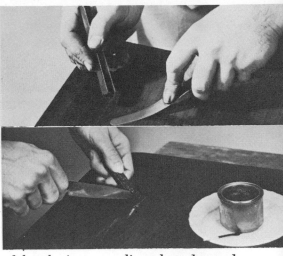

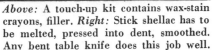

Above: A touch-up kit contains wax-stain crayons, filler. *Right:* Stick shellac has to be melted, pressed into dent, smoothed. Any bent table knife does this job well.

The proper treatment of splintered breaks is a complicated art learned by experience. If the piece of furniture is valuable, and there are any doubts about repairing such breaks, the job should be given to a cabinetmaker or an experienced restorer.

Broken turnings—legs, stretchers, and spindles—usually can be repaired with dowels and glue. When the break in a stretcher or rail is near the end, it should be glued first. Then a slightly oversized hole should be drilled for the dowel through the leg and across the glue joint, making it long enough so that the dowel will be countersunk. Then the glued dowel should be driven into the hole and clamped until the glue dries. The dowel should be masked with a wood plug, wood putty, or stick shellac.

When the break is near the middle, a small brad is driven into the center of one side of the break and the ends pushed together so that the head of the brad makes an impression on the other side of the break. With the brad holes as guides, holes are drilled in each side of the break for a dowel, the glued dowel is inserted in one side, both surfaces are coated with glue, and the break is clamped together. Since the holes may not form a perfectly straight line, they should be drilled slightly oversized for the dowel.

Most furniture repairs are simpler than those just outlined. Corner blocks should be checked and reglued if necessary; screws, when present, should be tightened. Breaks in flat members can be reinforced with a double wedge of hardwood glued in a mortise cut out to match. If a leg, rocker, or arm of a chair is missing or definitely beyond repair, it can usually be replaced by a new member shaped to match. Only a few common hand tools are needed to shape almost any part other than a turning which, of course, requires a wood lathe, but if these are not available a local woodworking shop is the solution. Matching the wood of an old piece presents a problem if the wood is fashioned from old-growth stock which is harder and more dense than present-day hardwoods cut from younger trees. A satisfactory match of the new to the old may require some searching.

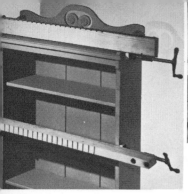

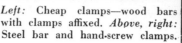

Left: Cheap clamps—wood bars with clamps affixed. *Above, right:* Steel bar and hand-screw clamps.

Although the many types of commercial clamps are easiest to use, a simple tourniquet can be used for many furniture clamping jobs. It is important that tension be applied directly across the joint being glued and not at an angle.

Ordinarily, all loose veneer should be reglued before the old finish is removed. This is not much of a problem near edges. The veneer is simply pried up and held in this position with a thin wooden wedge. As much of the old glue is scraped off as possible; then new glue is applied and spread with a toothpick or length of wire, and weight is applied to hold the veneer in place until the glue dries. A bag of sand makes an excellent weight for use on curved surfaces because it distributes the weight evenly. The veneer can be made more pliable if the loose portion is covered with a moistened cloth and a hot iron is then applied for a few moments. However, it is important not to soften the glue which is still holding in adjacent areas.

To repair blisters in veneer, cut them open down the center with a razor blade (following the grain) and wedge up the sides, one at a time, so that glue can be forced underneath. It is usually a good idea to use the method previously described to make the veneer more pliable when treating blisters. Once new glue has been applied, weights can be used to hold the veneer in place until the glue has set.

Replacing missing portions of veneer is a little more difficult, because the grain and color of the patch should match the rest of the surface. However, veneers are available in wide selections and variations of grain so that in most cases a matching piece can be obtained. Trim off irregular edges of the old veneer and cut the patch so that it fits exactly. This takes time, but if the result is a perfect fit the time has been well spent. When the fit is certain, glue is applied; then the patch is clamped or weighted in place until the glue dries.

Left: Cabinet clamps, which need some padding. Band clamps, as used for curves, with metal band (*center*), canvas band (*right*).

To lift shallow dents, carefully remove the varnish from the dented surface to expose the bare wood. Sometimes, a few drops of water applied to the bare wood will cause the compressed fibers to swell so that they will return to their original level.

If simple soaking does not work, heat can be tried. The wood is moistened as before. Then, after the water has penetrated the fibers, a pad is put over the dent and heat is applied with an iron. The iron must be lifted frequently to check progress, and when the dent has been lifted, the surface is stained and finished to match the surrounding area.

One way to take the warp out of a table leaf is to cause it to warp in the opposite direction. This can be done by laying a piece of carpet on the concave side, and dampening it with hot water. The convex side should be kept dry with plenty of room for air to circulate freely. Fibers on the concave side will absorb moisture and expand. A close watch must be kept on the progress of this intentional warping. When the leaf is straight, it should be clamped securely until it dries. If the leaf warps too far, the same procedure is followed to straighten it.

Another way, which generally is more certain to produce a satisfactory result, is to remove the warped piece and run a series of saw cuts, or kerfs, on the convex face. The kerfs are run to a depth of about three-fourths the thickness of the stock, stopping just short of cutting out at the ends, and are spaced about one-half inch apart. The kerfs cut through the fibers, and thus release the stresses which caused the piece to warp or cup. These cuts must be made either with a portable electric saw or a table saw. If neither is available, the job should be given to a cabinetmaker or lumber dealer.

NEW RUSH SEATS

A further challenge awaits the refinisher in creating new furniture and working with totally different materials.

Weaving new rush seats for ladder-back, Hitchcock, and other fine old period chairs on which this type of seat is commonly found is not difficult. The average-size chair seat takes about one-and-a-half pounds of cattail rush, which is available from any dealer in chair-seating materials.

Placing the rushes in water and letting them soak overnight makes them soft and pliable. Before they are used, the excess water and air should be wrung out, preferably by running the rushes through an ordinary washing-machine wringer. The rushes should make a crackling sound while being wrung out, which indicates that they are just right for twisting.

The first step in weaving rush is perhaps the most important. The diagrams should be studied carefully beforehand to acquaint the finisher with the start of the weaving pattern. With the chair facing him, the finisher selects two rushes, one tip and butt length. (The tip is the top growth and the butt is the stalk of the rush). He twists the middle section of the two

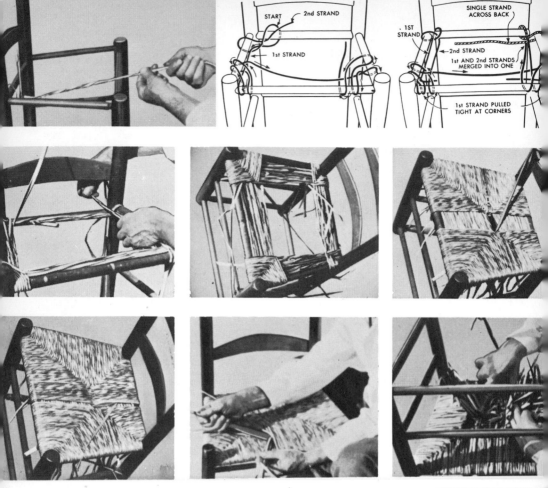

To weave rush seats first soak rushes until soft and pliable. Twist together the butt and tip ends of two strands. Loop this one longer strand over back rung and proceed to weave as shown above. Only one half of the strand is worked at a time; the other is tied off temporarily. Keeping it tightly twisted, work one strand from back corner through front corners to right rear. Tie off while second strand is carried through the same way. Then twist together. Complete the right back weave and carry to starting point *as one strand*. There they separate, begin same weave again. When the center gets too small for hands, a stuffing tool (*left*) will pull rushes through slits.

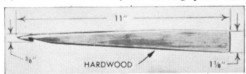

strands and loops them over the back rung of the seat frame, temporarily fastening one-half of the length to the chair back. When it is necessary to splice in a new rush to the strands being worked, he inserts it between the others, using either the tip or butt to keep the strand of uniform diameter.

The working end of the strand is kept twisted tightly and brought over the front rung at the left post, then down around and up through the frame and over the left side rung. The same wrapping step is repeated twice, then the twisted strand is continued across to the opposite rung. Here it is wrapped around the rung, up through the frame, around the front rung twice, and finally is carried to the rear post, where it is tied.

Going back to the starting point, he proceeds with the other half of the strand. The finisher weaves it around the left rear corner post; then, following the same procedure as before, he ends where he left off with the first half of the twisted strands. At this point, the two halves are merged and continued as one strand, passing over and around the rear rung, up through the frame, around the side rung, then back across to the starting point at the rear left-hand post.

In bringing the strand forward again, it is first divided into two halves as before. Then one is brought to the front; it is wrapped around the rungs at the corner exactly as was done with the starting strand, except that the second and subsequent strands are wrapped around the rungs only once. At the right rear post, the strands are merged into one, which is passed around the rungs and brought back to the starting point.

Each time around, one strand is added across the back, two along the sides, and two across the front. This is done to build out the slanting sides of the seat twice as fast at the front rung as at the back. This step is repeated until the center opening in the seat takes on a square shape, after which a single strand is used to go around the opening until it is filled.

The sides, which are shorter, generally close up first, and when this point is reached the weaving strands are merely run back and forth from front to back rungs in the form of a figure eight, passing them under at the center opening in the seat. The strands should be kept closely pushed together as they are wrapped around the rungs, and the top strands should be kept under slight tension and twisted tightly. As the center opening in the seat gradually closes up, it is helpful to use a wooden hook shaped like an oversize crochet hook to pull the strands through the narrow opening. After the weaving is completed, the loose ends which protrude from the bottom of the seat are snipped off.

Chairs with side rungs higher than the front rungs should have stuffing (scraps of rush) inserted in the side and front sections. The finisher adds this from the top when refilling the sides, and, from underneath, to stuff the front. The rear section is not stuffed.

The seat should be varnished as soon as it is completed. A good grade of clear varnish should be used. It should be applied to both top and bottom surfaces of the seat.

REUPHOLSTERING WITH FOAM RUBBER

No complicated assembly of springs and layers of padding is involved in upholstering with foam rubber. By following the basic steps shown in the accompanying photos, anyone who can use a pair of scissors and a stapling gun should be able to turn out a professional-looking job.

Foam rubber is available in various thicknesses by the foot, and also in molded shapes. It can be used in place of other materials for padding hard surfaces or topping spring cushions. When more than the normal depth of two inches is required, the thicker-cored utility stock (four inches and up) should be used. All of the materials and tools shown are easily obtainable from most department stores and mail-order houses.

Remove padding, webbing (*center*) from old chair (*left*), then staple new webbing (*right*). *Below left:* trace patterns on paper; *center*, add a half inch, cut and bevel foam rubber.

Above right: Cement muslin tacking strips to foam rubber. *Below: left*, pull strips tight, staple to frame; *center*, cover chair with upholstering fabric, and the job is completed. *Far right:* Electric scissors make cutting heavy upholstering fabrics quicker and easier.

Another *Popular Mechanics* book which you will want to own is

ALL ABOUT UPHOLSTERING

by John Bergen

This book will teach you how to *save hundreds* of *dollars* at the same time as you fill your home with new-looking furniture.

ALL ABOUT UPHOLSTERING not only carefully tells you, but actually *shows* you how each step in the job should be done. More than 300 drawings, charts, and photographs show exactly the best tools and materials to use and how to use them to do the best possible job in every situation.

Whether you use old stand-bys or the newest synthetics, you will find ALL ABOUT UPHOLSTERING the perfect guide for your job — from the first application of webbing, through placing springs, burlap, padding, up to the final covering and trim.

HAWTHORN BOOKS, INC.

70 Fifth Ave.   New York City 10011

Printed in the U.S.A. (4)

Before applying remover to any metal scrape off rust. Following stripping patch where needed and sand off.

WORKING WITH METAL

Most of the rules for refinishing wood also hold true for refinishing metal. However, there are a few additional points to keep in mind when working with metal, regardless of whether the refinishing job involved is a kitchen cabinet, a tricycle, or patio furniture.

A no-rinse remover is considered best for wood, generally because it eliminates the chance of raising the grain when rinsing. However, tests have shown that a water-rinse remover is much more efficient for baked-on enamel finishes on metals. Since the metal has no grain, this is the preferred type.

Follow the same procedure for applying the remover as for wood finishes, but take off any loose rust with a wire brush before the remover is used. Making sure that the metal is thoroughly dry before proceeding with finishing will prevent corrosion.

Both aluminum oxide and silicon carbide abrasives work well on metal. *Emery*, another abrasive, is a natural mineral of the aluminum oxide family, and for many years emery cloth was considered the best available material for finishing metals. It is still good for removing rust spots and other light work but, as a rule, one of the cloth-backed, aluminum-oxide abrasives which are specifically designed for use on metal will be much more satisfactory.

Crocus, which is cloth-backed, is a superfine abrasive, intended only for polishing metals which are not to be coated with an opaque finish such as enamel or lacquer. Metals polished to a high sheen should be protected with a clear metal lacquer. Metal which is to be coated with enamels or colored lacquers should not be polished. Rather, the surface should be abraded with a fine aluminum-oxide abrasive to provide a good bonding surface for the new finish.

Quite often the old finish is in reasonably good condition. In such cases, after the surface is cleaned and abraded lightly, it should be given a single coat of enamel. Here is where the spray gun, or the aerosol-packaged enamels, prove really worthwhile in producing a professional finish in a matter of minutes. A coat of enamel or lacquer can be sprayed over almost any previous finish on metal which has been there long enough to completely oxidize.

Painting cupboards in the kitchen, ironwork outside, is very simple with easy-to-handle aerosol spraying cans.

For brush application, try a fast-drying synthetic. One of the self-leveling lacquers or four-hour enamels will give excellent results. If the old finish and rust have to be removed from the metal, and nicks and scratches need to be abraded, a metal primer should be sprayed on as the first coat, followed with enamel or lacquer.

When finishing cast iron, from which the surfacer has been removed, such as parts of your power tools, primer-surfacer should be used to insure a good job. This material is self-leveling and will fill any small scratches and the rough surface left by the sand mold. It provides a good bond to the iron and a smooth base for the top-coat enamel. Primer-surfacers are either lacquer or synthetic products, and are almost pastelike. They are still quite heavy, even after reducing, but they spray smoothly even with light-duty guns.

If, in removing the old finish from iron, holes or low spots are encountered, they can be filled with a lacquer putty which is specially prepared for the purpose. This product is used as it comes from the container. It is applied and smoothed with a putty knife. After thorough drying, the combined primer-surfacer and putty coat is ready for sanding, using wet-or-dry paper with water as a lubricant. It is best to start with 3/0 grit and finish off with 6/0 grit. The slush should be cleaned off with a soft rag and wiped dry.

As many as three to five coats of surfacer may be needed to smooth up a cast-iron surface, especially if it is badly pitted by rust. Each coat should be sanded until the bare metal shows through in the high spots. This is not as hard as it sounds, because the surfacer sands quite easily without clogging the abrasive.

If several coats of surfacer are required, two different colors should be used so that low spots can be easily detected. Deeper depressions should be filled with several coats, each coat being feathered by sanding until the surface is level. In this way, the patch will bond firmly to the metal.

Before the finish is applied, make certain that there are no large breaks to bare metal in the primer-surfacer coat. With a good foundation, one coat of enamel or lacquer should be sufficient. If a second coat of lacquer is applied, the first coat should be sanded lightly with 5/0 wet-or-dry paper. Even though the finish is sanded through to bare metal here and there, no harm will be done, because the second coat will catch any spots where metal has been bared.

The prime enemy of outdoor iron or steel furniture is rust. Therefore, when refinishing, it is important to clean and abrade all surfaces to remove rust pits, If rusting is particularly bad, a special, penetrating-type rust preventer is best as a first coat. House paint should not be used on metal patio or lawn furniture. Many such products are formulated to chalk when weathered and will rub off on clothing. An exterior grade of enamel or a lacquer will not chalk.

A number of interesting textures and color combinations especially well-suited for use on metal are described below, but, before any one of these is attempted, a sample of the finish should be tried on a small metal panel. Most of these are best used for smaller pieces.

Crackle enamel is available either clear or in standard colors, and is sprayed over a lacquer undercoat. It sets almost instantly and is formulated to shrink on drying. It is this property that causes the film to crack, or crackle, into numerous small irregular sections, exposing the lacquer undercoat. Red crackle over black lacquer is commonly used to produce a Spanish varqueno or Oriental effect. Usually the instructions will direct that the undercoat be completely dry before the crackle coat is sprayed on. The lighter this coat is applied, the smaller the cracks will be. A little practice is needed in order to get uniform crackle texture over a large surface.

For a pleasing transparent effect, clear crackle enamel (ten parts) can be mixed with the desired color (about one part) ; for example, a base coat of clear lacquer or a rich gold. For an imitation leather finish, a coat of

brown lacquer should be sprayed over the crackle surface. In all cases, the crackle coat should be protected when dry with a thin spray-coat of clear lacquer.

Wrinkle lacquer is one of the most popular finishes for metal. It is somewhat heavier than the average spraying lacquer, and is best applied with a pressure-feed gun, preferably external mix. However, some wrinkle finishes are formulated especially for brushing, and it is especially important to read the instructions before applying.

Like most texture finishes, a thick coat gives a heavy, pronounced pattern, while a thin coat yields a more finely-textured effect. A medium-heavy coat usually proves the most satisfactory.

Many of these finishes must be baked in an oven at a temperature between 180° and 220° F. The baking time runs about two hours at 220°. Air-dry products are also available, but mild heat from a heat lamp, or even direct sunlight, produces a somewhat more durable and uniform finish. The wrinkle finish can be top-coated with a light spray-coat of enamel, if desired.

"Jack-Frost" lacquer, also called prismatic lacquer, comes in many colors, both opaque and also transparent. Apply a heavy coat directly over bare metal, and the texture will start to form in about two minutes. Such a finish is especially effective on a highly polished surface. One form of this

finish can be applied to glass to make it translucent.

A process known as *smutting*, which is similar to glazing, adds depth to the Jack-Frost finish. After the textured surface coated with a colored Jack-Frost lacquer has dried, a smut from colored pigment should be mixed in japan or oil and turpentine. Ordinary paint or enamel can also be used. A coat of the smutting color should be applied over the lacquer and immediately wiped with a clean rag. This will leave the smut color in depressed portions, adding depth to the finish.

Metallic powders can be mixed with almost any kind of clear varnish or lacquer. The best vehicle for spray application is a water-white lacquer. One tablespoon of powder to one pint of lacquer will cover well. These solutions will not keep; therefore, only enough solution for the job at hand should be mixed.

Glossary*

Annual growth ring—The layer grown in a single year, including the spring-wood and summerwood.

Bar top—Indicates proof against alcohol, heat, cold, etc. Used for table and bar tops.

Bark—Outer layer of a tree, comprised of the inner bark, or thin, inner living part (phloem) and the outer bark, or corky layer, composed of dry, dead tissue.

Bending, steam—The process of forming curved wood members by steaming or boiling the wood and bending it to a form.

Bird's-eye—Small localized areas in wood with the fibers indented or otherwise contorted to form small circular or elliptical figures remotely resembling birds' eyes on the tangential surface. Used for decorative purposes. Fairly common in sugar maple, it is comparatively rare in other hardwood species.

Bleaching—Bleaching lacquer is simply a water-white, thin lacquer, the kind of finish which is required on extremely light-color woods.

Blonding—A thin white lacquer used to obtain blond tone. Can be made by adding one part white lacquer to four or five parts clear lacquer.

Bow or wind—The distortion in a board that deviates from flatness length-wise but not across its faces.

Broad-leaved trees—(See *Hardwoods.*)

Brushing—A slow-drying lacquer suitable for application with a soft brush. Should be thinned with a slow-drying thinner for best results, but often sold at brushing consistency.

Cambium—The one-cell-thick layer of tissue between the bark and wood that repeatedly subdivides to form new wood and bark cells.

Catalyst finishes—Hard, tough finishes which are proof against steam, alcohol, etc. Used for table tops. Requires catalyst (hardener) which is mixed with synthetic before use. One to four hours to dry.

---

* Wood terms courtesy of United States Forest Service

Cell—A general term for the minute units of wood structure, including wood fibers, vessel members, and other elements of diverse structure and function.

Check—A lengthwise separation, or split, of the wood, usually extending across the rings of annual growth and commonly resulting from stresses set up in the wood during seasoning.

Clear flat—A clear lacquer which dries flat. Can be intermixed with a similar-brand gloss lacquer.

Clear gloss—A clear lacquer which dries with a glossy finish; thinned with lacquer thinner. Must be sprayed; dries too quickly for brushing. Dries dust-free in a few minutes; one to two hours to recoat.

Collapse—The flattening of groups of cells in heartwood during the drying or pressure treatment of wood, characterized by a caved-in or corrugated appearance.

Crook—The distortion in a board that deviates flatwise from a straight line across the width of the board.

Decay—The decomposition of wood substance by fungi. *Advanced* (or *typical*) *decay*—The older stage of decay in which the destruction is readily recognized because the wood has become punky, soft and spongy, stringy, ringshaked, pitted, or crumbly. Decided discoloration or bleaching of the rotted wood is often apparent. *Incipient decay*—The early stage of decay that has not proceeded far enough to soften or otherwise perceptibly impair the hardness of the wood. It is usually accompanied by a slight discoloration or bleaching of the wood.

Density—The weight of a body per unit volume. When expressed in the c. g. s. (centimeter-grain-second) system, it is numerically equal to the specific gravity of the same substance.

Dewaxed shellac—A superfine, bleached, and dewaxed shellac, commonly used as the basis for various kinds of French varnish.

Diffuse-porous wood—Certain hardwoods in which the pores tend to be uniform in size and distribution throughout each annual ring, or to decrease in size slightly and gradually toward the outer border of the ring.

Dimension—(See *Lumber*)

Dimension stock—A term largely superseded by the term *hardwood dimension lumber*. It is hardwood stock processed to a point where the maximum waste is left at a dimension mill, and the maximum utility is delivered to the user. It is stock of specified thickness, width, and length, in multiples thereof. According to specification, it may be solid or glued; rough or surfaced; semi-fabricated or completely fabricated.

Dimensional stabilization—Reduction through special treatment in swelling and shrinking of wood, caused by changes in its moisture content with changes in relative humidity.

Dry kiln—(See *Kiln*)

Dry rot—A term loosely applied to any dry, crumbly rot, but especially to that which, when in an advanced stage, permits the wood to be crushed easily to a dry powder. The term is actually a misnomer, since all wood-rotting fungi require considerable moisture for growth.

Early wood—(See *Springwood*)

Edge-grained—(See *Grain*)

Extractives—Substances in wood which are not an integral part of the cellular structure and can be removed by solution in hot or cold water, ether, benzene, or other solvents that do not react chemically with wood components.

Fiber, wood—A comparatively long (from one twenty-fifth of an inch or less to one-third inch), narrow, tapering wood cell, closed at both ends.

Figure—The pattern produced in a wood surface by annual growth rings, rays, knots, deviations from regular grain (such as interlocked and wavy grain), and irregular coloration.

Flakes—(See *Rays, wood*)

Flat-grained—(See *Grain*)

Grade—The designation of the quality of a manufactured piece of wood or of logs.

Grain—The direction, size, arrangement, appearance, or quality of the elements in wood or lumber. To have a specific meaning the term must be qualified. *Close-grained wood*—Wood with narrow, inconspicuous annual rings. The term is sometimes used to designate wood having small and closely-spaced pores, but in this sense the term "fine-textured" is more often used. *Coarse-grained wood*—Wood with wide conspicuous annual rings in which there is considerable difference between springwood and summerwood. The term is sometimes used to designate wood with large pores, such as oak, ash, chestnut, or walnut, but in this sense the term "coarse-textured" is more often used. *Cross-grained wood*—Wood in which the fibers deviate from a line parallel to the sides of the piece. Cross grain may be either diagonal or spiral grain, or a combination of the two. *Curly-grained wood*—Wood in which the fibers are distorted so that they have a curled appearance, as in "bird's-eye" wood. The areas showing curly grain may vary up to several inches in diameter. *Diagonal-grained wood*—Wood in which the annual rings are at angle with the axis of a piece as a result of sawing at an angle with the bark of the tree or log. It is considered a form of cross grain. *Edge-grained wood*—(See *Grain, close-grained wood*). *Flat-grained lumber*—Wood that has been sawed so that the wide surfaces extend approximately parallel to the annual growth rings. Lumber is considered flat grained when the annual growth rings make an angle of less than 45° with the surface of the piece. *Interlocked-grained wood*—Wood in which the fibers are inclined in one direction in a number of rings of annual growth, then gradually reverse and are inclined in an opposite direction in succeeding growth rings, then reverse again. *Open-grained wood*—Common classification by painters for woods with large pores, such as oak, ash, chestnut, and walnut. Also known as "coarse-textured." *Plain-sawed lumber*—Another term for flat-grained lumber. *Quarter-sawed lumber*—Another term for edge-grained lumber. *Spiral-grained wood*—Wood in which the fibers take a spiral course about the trunk of a tree instead of the normal vertical course. The spiral may extend in a right-hand or left-hand direction around the tree trunk. Spiral grain is a form of cross grain. *Straight-grained wood*—Wood in which the fibers run parallel to the axis of a piece. *Vertical-grained lumber*—Another term for edge-grained lumber. *Wavy-grained wood*—Wood in which the fibers collectively take the form of waves or undulations.

Green—Freshly-sawed lumber, or lumber that has received no intentional drying; unseasoned. The term does not apply to lumber that may have become completely wet through waterlogging.

Hardwoods—Generally, the botanical group of trees that have broad leaves, in contrast to the conifers or softwoods. The term has no reference to the actual hardness of the wood.

Heartwood—The wood extending from the pith to the sapwood, the cells of which no longer participate in the life processes of the tree. Heartwood may be infiltrated with gums, resins, and other materials that usually make it darker and more decay-resistant than sapwood.

Honeycombing—Checks, which are often not visible at the surface, but occur in the interior of a piece of wood, usually along the wood rays.

Joint—The junction of two pieces of wood or veneer.

Kiln—A heated chamber for drying lumber, veneer, and other wood products.

Knot—That portion of a branch or limb which has been surrounded by subsequent growth of the wood of the trunk or other portion of the tree. As a knot appears on the sawed surface, it is merely a section of the entire knot, its shape depending upon the direction of the cut.

Longitudinal—Generally, the direction along the length of the grain of wood.

Lumber—The product of the saw and planing mill, not further manufactured than by sawing, re-sawing, passing lengthwise through a standard planing machine, cross-cutting to length, and matching. *Boards*—Yard lumber less than two inches thick and one or more inches wide. *Dimension*—Lumber from two inches to, but not including, five inches thick, and two or more inches wide. *Dressed size*—The dimensions of lumber after shrinking from the green dimensions and being surfaced with a planing machine to three-eighths or one-half inch less than the nominal or rough size. For example, a two-by-four-inch stud actually measures one-and-five-eighths by three-and-five-eighths inches under American lumber standards for softwood lumber. *Nominal size* —As applied to timber or lumber, the rough-sawed commercial size by which it is known and sold in the market. *Structural lumber*—Lumber that is two or more inches thick and four or more inches wide, intended for use where working stresses are required. The grading of structural lumber is based on the strength of the piece and the use of the entire piece. *Timber*—Lumber five or more inches in its least dimension. Beams, stringers, posts, caps, sills, girders, purlins, etc., may be classified as timber.

Medullary rays—(See *Rays, wood*)

Moisture content—The amount of water contained in the wood. Usually expressed as a percentage of the weight of the oven-dry wood.

Naval stores—A term applied to the oils, resins, tars, and pitches derived from oleoresin contained in, exuded by, or extracted from, trees chiefly of the pine species (genus *Pinus*) or from the wood of such trees.

Non-lifting—Non-lifting lacquers are intended for refinishing over varnish. The solvent commonly used has high alcohol content; if reduction is required a non-lifting (high alcohol) thinner should be used.

Old growth—Timber growing in, or harvested from, a mature, naturally-established forest. When the trees have grown most or all of their individual lives in active competition with their companions for sunlight and moisture, the timber is usually straight and relatively free of knots.

Orange—The natural shellac color; suitable for all dark woods.

Oven-dry wood—Wood dried to constant weight in an oven at temperatures above that of boiling water (usually 101° to 105°C. or 214° to 221°F.).

Pale Rubbing and Polishing—See (*Rubbing and polishing*)

Peck—Pockets or areas of disintegrated wood caused by advanced stages of localized decay in the living tree. It is usually associated with cypress and incense-cedar. Peck develops no further once lumber is seasoned.

Penetrating floor sealer—A penetrating finish for floors, but also good for simple finish on furniture. Apply to bare wood only; brush, mop, or spray. Low luster. Usually steel-wooled and then waxed.

Pitch pocket—An opening that extends parallel to the annual growth rings and that contains, or has contained, either solid or liquid pitch.

Pitch streak—A well-defined accumulation of pitch in a more or less regular streak in the wood of certain softwoods.

Pith—The small, soft core occurring in the structural center of a tree trunk, branch, twig, or log.

Plain-sawed—(See *Grain*)

Plywood—An assembly made of layers (plies) of veneer, or of veneer in combination with a lumber core, joined with an adhesive. The grain of adjoining plies, usually an odd number to obtain balanced construction, is laid at right angles.

Plywood sealer—Especially good for equalizing hard and soft areas in fir and pine. Clear amber; also available in white for blond effects.

Polishing varnish—Has a shorter oil content than regular. Although it polishes nicely, it tends to be brittle, and should be used only as a top coat over regular rubbing varnish.

Pore—(See *Vessels*)

Porous woods—Another name for hardwoods, which frequently have vessels or pores large enough to be seen readily without magnification.

Preservative—Any substance that is effective, for a reasonable length of time, in preventing the development and action of wood-rotting fungi, borers of various kinds, and harmful insects that deteriorate wood.

Quarter-sawed—(See *Grain*)

Radial—Coincident with a radius from the axis of the tree or log to the circumference. A radial section is a lengthwise section in a plane that extends from pith to bark.

Rate of growth—The rate at which a tree has laid on wood, measured radially in the trunk or in lumber cut from the trunk. The unit of measure in use is the number of annual growth rings per inch.

Rays, wood—Strips of cells extending radially within a tree and varying in height from a few cells in some species to four or more inches in oak. The rays serve primarily to store food and transport it horizontally in the tree.

Resin passage (or *duct*)—Intercellular passages that contain and transmit resinous materials. On a cut surface, they are usually inconspicuous. They may extend vertically parallel to the axis of the tree or at right angles to the axis and parallel to the rays.

Ring-porous woods—A group of hardwoods in which the pores are comparatively large at the beginning of each annual ring and decrease in size more or less abruptly toward the outer portion of the ring, thus forming a distinct inner zone of pores, known as the springwood, and an outer zone with smaller pores, known as the summerwood.

Rubbed effect—A varnish which dries to a satin finish resembling hand-rubbed work. Best used for top coat only; use regular gloss varnish for undercoats. Also, in reference to lacquer, a semi-gloss.

Rubbing and Polishing—Varnish designed specifically for furniture finishing. It contains less oil than other varnishes, and is generally described as a short-oil varnish. Short-oil varnishes sand and polish with a minimum of gumming. Drying time is usually 24 to 48 hours. Four-hour drying products are also available. *Pale rubbing and polishing* is made very clear for light-color finishes. There is also a lacquer made especially for rubbing and polishing; generally, simply the better grades of lacquer. Usually water-white. Also called piano-finishing lacquer.

Sanding Sealer—Contains a sanding agent which permits clean, easy sanding. One hour to sand. Also, in reference to varnishes, a sealer designed for a first coating over stain or filler; usually a brushing lacquer or a shellac base sealer, either of which can be used under any kind of varnish.

Sap—All the fluids in a tree except special secretions and excretions, such as oleoresin.

Sapwood—The living wood of pale color near the outside of the log. Under most conditions the sapwood is more susceptible to decay than heartwood.

Seasoning—Removing moisture from green wood in order to improve its serviceability. *Air-dried*—Dried by exposure to air, usually in a yard, without artificial heat. *Kiln-dried*—Dried in a kiln with the use of artificial heat.

Second growth—Timber that has grown after removal of all or a large part of the previous stand by cutting, fire, wind, or other agency.

Shellac mixing—A lacquer which mixes with shellac, giving increased resistance to water and better sanding qualities.

Softwoods—Generally, the botanical group of trees that bear cones and in most cases have needlelike or scalelike leaves; also the wood produced by such trees. The term has no reference to the actual hardness of the wood.

Spar—Long-oil content, dark, slow-drying, moderate gloss varnishes. The long-oil content makes this varnish tough and elastic. Used for exterior work; sometimes called marine varnish. Dries hard in 12 to 24 hours.

Specific gravity—The ratio of the weight of a body to the weight of an equal volume of water at 4°C., or other specified temperature.

Springwood—The portion of the annual growth ring that is formed during the early part of the season's growth. In most softwoods and in ring-porous hardwoods, it is less dense and weaker mechanically than is summerwood.

Stain—A discoloration in wood that may be caused by such diverse agencies as micro-organisms, metal, or chemicals. The term also applies to materials used to color wood.

Strength—The term in its broader sense includes all the properties of wood that enable it to resist different forces or loads. In its more restricted sense, strength may apply to any one of the mechanical properties, in which event the name of the property under consideration should be stated, thus: strength in compression parallel to grain, strength in bending, hardness, and so on.

Stress—Force per unit of area.

Summerwood—The portion of the annual growth ring that is formed after the springwood formation has ceased. In most softwoods and in ring-porous hardwoods, it is denser and stronger mechanically than springwood.

Table top—A hard and tough varnish, proof against heat, cold, and alcohol. Usually a synthetic. Four-hour dry.

Tangential—In a strict sense, coincident with a tangent at the circumference of a tree or log, or parallel to such a tangent. In practice, however, it often means roughly coincident with a growth ring. A tangential section is a longitudinal section through a tree or limb and is perpendicular to a radius. Flat-grained and plain-sawed lumber is sawed tangentially.

Texture—A term often used interchangeably with grain. Sometimes used to combine the concepts of density and degree of contrast between springwood and summerwood.

Twist—A distortion caused by the turning or winding of the edges of a board so that the four corners of any face are no longer in the same plane.

Tyloses—Masses of cells appearing somewhat like froth in the pores of some hardwoods, notably in white oak and black locust. In hardwoods, tyloses are formed when walls of living cells which surround vessels extend into the vessels. They are sometimes formed in softwoods in a similar manner by the extension of cell walls into resin-passage cavities.

Varnish stain—General-purpose interior varnish tinted with dye colors or pigments. All wood colors. Stains and varnishes in one coat. Good for pine floors; seldom used on quality furniture except as quick refinish.

Veneer—A thin layer or sheet of wood cut on a veneer machine. *Rotary-cut veneer*—Veneer cut in a lathe which rotates a log or bolt, chucked in the center, against a knife. *Sawed veneer*—Veneer produced by sawing. *Sliced veneer*—Veneer that is sliced off a log, bolt, or flitch with a knife.

Vertical grain—(See *Grain*)

Vessels—Wood cells of comparatively large diameter that have open ends, and are set one above the other so as to form continuous tubes. The openings of the vessels on the surface of a piece of wood are usually referred to as pores.

Virgin growth—The original growth of mature trees.

Warp—Any variation from a true or plane surface. Warp includes bow, crook, cup, and twist, or any combination thereof.

Waterproof shellac—A modified shellac which is completely waterproof. Most products of this type are closer to being brushing lacquers than shellac.

Water white—Perfectly clear, water-white lacquer. Should be used for all blond finishes; also as a protective coating for art metals.

Weathering—The mechanical or chemical disintegration and discoloration of the surface of wood that is caused by exposure to light, the action of dust and sand carried by winds, and the alternate shrinking and swelling of the surface fibers with the continual variation in moisture content brought by changes in the weather. Weathering does not include decay.

White—Bleached flakes which produce a clear, transparent solution. This is the product most used for floors and furniture work.

Wood substance—The solid material of which wood is composed. It usually refers to the extractive-free solid substance of which the cell walls are composed, but this is not always true. There is no wide variation in chemical composition or specific gravity between the wood substance of the various species. The characteristic differences of species are largely due to differences in infiltrated materials and variations in relative amounts of cell walls and cell cavities.

Workability—The degree of ease and smoothness of cut obtainable with hand or machine tools.

Index

The Author and His Book

Arthur Mikesell was born in Ovid, Michigan, in 1932. After serving in the United States Army he returned to Michigan State University, from which he was graduated in 1957. For Popular Mechanics Magazine, *of which he is Associate Editor, he has written many articles on refinishing furniture and allied crafts.*

Mr. Mikesell first became interested in refinishing furniture because he had inherited eleven rooms crammed full of old furniture in need of refinishing. But when he read through all the available books on the subject, he discovered a distressing lack of good material. Nevertheless he set out to learn the craft and complete the job. Now, many years and eleven rooms later, Mr. Mikesell has decided to insure that others don't encounter the same problem he faced: he has written the book he couldn't find.

THE POPULAR MECHANICS HOME BOOK OF REFINISHING FUR-NITURE *(Hawthorn, 1963) was set in type by the Harry Sweetman Typesetting Corporation, New York City, printed by Universal Lithographers, Inc., Baltimore, Md. and bound by Chas. H. Bohn & Co., Inc., New York City. The body type is Bodoni, designed by Giambattista Bodoni of Parma.*

A HAWTHORN BOOK

The POPULAR MECHANICS Home Book of Refinishing Furniture

by Arthur Mikesell

THIS BOOK WILL SAVE YOU MONEY!

In your home's attic or cellar, aren't there many pieces of furniture going to waste? Perhaps some are dearly cherished, possessions of many years; perhaps some you know to be fine pieces of craftsmanship. Yet because wear has bruised and battered them, or because they no longer "fit" into your home's color-scheme, they lie unused, as good as discarded. *This is unnecessary waste!*

THIS BOOK WILL STOP WASTE AND SAVE FURNITURE!

THE POPULAR MECHANICS HOME BOOK OF RE-FINISHING FURNITURE shows exactly how to make an old, too-often repainted piece of furniture into one as lovely as the finest in any showroom — yet it need never leave your workroom! You *don't* have to pay a professional. You *don't* have to buy new furniture. You *can* save those old pieces that you love. *You can save that furniture and you can save money — and at the same time learn a wonderfully satisfying hobby.*

THE POPULAR MECHANICS HOME BOOK OF RE-FINISHING FURNITURE includes hundreds of photographs, diagrams, tables and charts and a clear, enjoyably readable text. These explain both general rules and specific projects, and show how to refinish and repair all kinds of wood and metal, and even how to reupholster. THE POPULAR MECHANICS HOME BOOK OF REFINISHING FURNITURE will delight both beginners and experts — the refinisher who merely wants to save a rusting outside chair, and the refinisher who spends all his time seeking and saving antique masterpieces hidden under the paint and grime of time.

In all cases this book begins at the beginning (even with the growth and milling of all kinds of lumber) and then carefully covers both the fundamentals and the most advanced tricks of the trade — the basics of stripping, sanding, repairing broken parts, sealing, refinishing, and the arts of hand-rubbed oiling, mixing special stains to fit unique colors, concealing blemishes, special bleachings.